PEOPLE OF THE TRUTH

ALSO BY ROBERT E. WEBBER

Worship Is a Verb
Worship Old and New
The Book of Family Prayer
The Church in the World
Evangelicals on the Canterbury Trail
Celebrating Our Faith
The Majestic Tapestry

PEOPLE
of the
TRUTH
The Power of the Worshiping
Community in the Modern World

ROBERT E. WEBBER
RODNEY CLAPP

Wipf and Stock Publishers
EUGENE, OREGON

Wipf and Stock Publishers
199 West 8th Avenue, Suite 3
Eugene, Oregon 97401

The People of the Truth
The Power of the Worshipping Community in the Modern World
By Webber, Robert E. and Clapp, Rodney
Copyright©1988 Webber, Robert E. and Clapp, Rodney
ISBN: 1-57910-560-2
Publication Date: February, 2001
Previously published by Harper and Row, 1988.

To the communities of St. Barnabas's (Glen Ellyn) and St. Mark's (Geneva), which give us hope that the church—however imperfect—can be what it is supposed to be.

Contents

Acknowledgments

For their generosity of time and mind, we owe much to Christopher Lutes and Phillip Ellsworth, who read and critiqued our first draft chapter by chapter; to David Neff and Andrea Lodge, who reviewed the manuscript as a whole; to Jane Marston for her clerical assistance; and to editors Robert D. San Souci and Roy M. Carlisle. Our wives, Joanne and Sandy, with their patience and encouragement, rendered the entire process tolerable and even rewarding.

PART ONE
THE LOSS OF STORY

[The Church] exists . . . to set up in the world a new sign which is radically dissimilar to [the world's] own manner and which contradicts it in a way which is full of promise. In all its creaturely impotence and human corruption, [the church] is required to do this.

—KARL BARTH, *CHURCH DOGMATICS*, IV/3.2

Introduction

In the past decade or so an extraordinary change has occurred in the interface between the two realms that are arguably America's most powerful and important: religion and politics.

The mainline "liberal" church that enjoyed ascendancy since the New Deal days of Franklin Roosevelt has been unseated. In its place the once despised and maligned fundamentalist church latched onto Ronald Reagan's coattails and created a new religio-political alliance. The arena of religious politicking that was the domain of sophisticated Protestant gentlemen has been commandeered by Bible-wielding evangelists.

We write as persons who have deep sympathies for both camps. One of us grew up fundamentalist; both of us were largely educated and have practiced our professions at institutions central to evangelicalism. As will be clear in the pages that follow, we do not disguise our debt to and continuing appreciation for that tradition. But we also have other affiliations. One of us grew up United Methodist; both of us are now confirmed Episcopalians. Although the mainline churches are currently characterized as "oldline" or "sideline," we find much to champion in the non-evangelical tradition as well.

It might be said that, drawing from evangelical and mainline traditions, we enjoy an embarrassment of riches. But that is not the case in the subject of interest at the moment, religion and politics. Like many Christians of all persuasions, we are dissatisfied (and sometimes mortified) with the religio-political power plays of the religious Right and the religious Left.

This book, then, is about the dilemma so many Christians face: what to do if you are an enthusiast for neither the New Right nor the Old Left but still take seriously the church's social and political responsibility. It is our conviction, and that of a growing number of significant Christian thinkers, that there is an alternative.

Christians need not believe that the root source of their political concern is this or that economic theory or one or another form of government. The church can assert that God is not a Marxist; he does not call us to the kingdom of socialism. And Christians need not believe that the problems of the world will be solved by rediscovered patriotism, by restored American imperialism, or by some combination of capitalism and democracy. The church can assert that God is not an American; he does not call us to the kingdom of Uncle Sam.

It is high time, in fact, that the church in America makes a priority of disavowing all the cultural, political, and economic ideologies it so eagerly associated with in a quest for illusory power and influence. Rather than attempting to reinstate its old triumphalism, the church should acknowledge that it lives in a largely de-Christianized situation. Then it should exploit that situation by contradicting the expectations of the world and worldly Christians. It should declare that civil religion is now a dead end practically as it always was theologically. And it should recover its *distinct* identity, an identity enacted and rehearsed in worship.

In short, the church should dare to lay down its life; to give up its ill-begotten political leverage; to turn aside from success and stop counting heads (or dollars); to stand at the side of the forgotten poor and oppressed; to be a sign and a witness of humanity's insufficiency and God's all-sufficiency.

Such contradiction is a contradiction bearing promise, because the only hope for this desperately hurting and divided world is not a political or economic program. It is the Christ proclaimed in the gospel and celebrated in worship. And the only people charged with proclaiming this Christ is the church, a people of the truth.

1. The Centrality of the Church

Throughout the history of America, politics and the church have conducted a strange, ambivalent relationship. Sometimes one has shunned the other; sometimes the two have embraced. But divorced or married, there has always been a tension between them. In this century, Christians of differing political persuasions have attempted to resolve the tension with religious-political alliances: the religious Left with the political Left, and—more recently—the religious Right with the political Right.

Although we believe Christians of both Left and Right have sought to act responsibly before God, there is a problem with their alliances. It is a problem of method. Both camps believe they must act politically, using the means of government to fulfill the highest Christian responsibilities of the day. It is as if Christians can do none of their most important business without the intermediary of law and government. And so the most visible pastors of our time, from Jesse Jackson to Jerry Falwell, have thrown their most vital efforts into influencing the political drift of the country. American Christianity seems to be fixated on a single question: "Is the United States what God wants it to be?"

When this becomes the primary question, it is clear there has been a move straight from the individual Christian to the nation America. That move is the theological equivalent of building a wheel without a hub: something essential has been left out of the middle. We want to suggest that the missing essential is the church.

Quite simply, the Christian's immediate concern should not be with the nation but with the church. The primary Christian question is not "Is the nation what God wants it to be?" but "How is the church? Is it what God wants it to be?"

The church at worship is the radical center from which a Christian political presence in the world radiates. Worship is central because it celebrates and reenacts the Christian story: the story of Christ come to suffer, then defeat, evil. When Christians worship they are shaped by this story; they become a corporate body formed in the image of Christ, called to heed the truth and live in a divided world as a sign of the future kingdom. But the story Christians reenact in worship is not like any story the world tells or celebrates, so the politics of the worshiping community is not the politics of any national government. Instead, it is the politics of the kingdom of God, eschewing power and legislative clout in favor of influence through service and respectful persuasion.

We are asserting that Christian influence in society should begin with the church, not with government. But to say that the church should concentrate first on itself seems to encourage withdrawal from the life-and-death predicaments confronting the nation and the wider world. It may appear that we are recommending Christians depart from politics and retreat to the cozy and undemanding confines of the family circle. That is emphatically not the case. We are not suggesting that Christians depart from the realm of politics and abandon (or even lessen) social concern. Rather, we are suggesting their politics and social concern are not radical enough. They are not radical enough because American Christians have come to depend on the nation, rather than the church, as their *primary* instrument of social change and communal influence.

Can the church concentrate first (though not solely) on its worship and its mission without withdrawing from wider society, without dwindling into an ineffectual and sectarian body? It can, we believe, because such concentration will yield the church's true identity and vision, what the church really is and how it can see the world for what it really is. By recognizing and reaffirming its own distinctive identity and vision, the church can in fact be a more potent social and political presence than it now is.

The church gains its distinctive vision and identity from its story, and, as we have said, it learns its story in its worship. But American Christians now polarized toward the political Right or Left, and caught up in their respective programs, will not be persuaded to look more deeply to story and worship until they have recognized three preceding realities: first, that the faith or story of the church goes beyond individualism; second, that Christianity is both individual (personal) and social; and third, that worship is ultimately itself a special kind of politics—what we will call "depth politics."

BEYOND INDIVIDUALISM

A friend who pastored a church in Green Bay, Wisconsin, tells us of an elderly man named Wilson, a gentleman he met while visiting neighborhood homes. The old man informed the young pastor that he had just become a Christian—all by himself. It was done, he boasted, simply by reading the Bible. The implication was that Wilson hardly needed a church. If he could find Jesus without a church, why consider joining one after he had Jesus? This was a point of considerable pride to the old man. All his life he had lived without needing or depending on any other man or woman. Wilson was convinced the best way to do anything was independently, without help from or debt to anyone—anyone on earth, at least.

Ironically, the illusion the gentleman from Green Bay labors under is not at all unusual. In America, it is most widely shared, a "powerful cultural friction that we not only can, but must, make up our deepest beliefs in the isolation of our private selves."[1] It has unavoidably affected the way American Christians understand their faith.

Most significantly, individualism narrows faith by making the church, the worshiping community, a kind of vestigial organ. Like the appendix, the church is there, but American Christians aren't quite sure why. If necessary, they can remove it and get along quite well without it. But individualistic Christians go even further and say of the church what they would never say of the appendix: that they may get along *better* without it. The church is actually put at odds with a "personal relationship" to God.

As one Christian told Robert Bellah and his fellow sociologists, Christ will "come into your heart" without any church at all.[2] This man was not simply making the point that the church does not control Christ (nothing could be truer); he was implicitly criticizing the church, which he considered hypocritical and perhaps stifling. Like Wilson of Green Bay, he neglected the historical fact that knowledge and understanding of Christ was initiated in and passed down by a community, in the fashion of what Bellah calls the "traditional pattern." Within the traditional pattern there is "a certain priority of the religious community over the individual. The community exists before the individual is born and will continue after his or her death. The relationship of the individual to God is ultimately personal, but it is mediated by the whole pattern of community life."[3]

It is the sense and appreciation of the mediating community that seems lost in much American Christianity. American Christians unfortunately believe the best way to live the Christian life is like a deep sea diver, with a private hose linked directly to the source of grace, operating in isolation from other Christians.[4] Certainly there is a commendable sense in which all Christians can say they have, as one woman told Bellah, "a commitment to God that is beyond church." But the same woman betrays the insidious quality of her individualism when she elaborates and subtly puts God against the church: "I felt my relationship with God was O.K. when I wasn't with the church."[5]

In this all too common view, the church exists exclusively as a personal support—perhaps a place to go when the private diving hose needs mending. The focus is not on seeing the gospel proclaimed, seeing a community of God's people built, seeing the hungry and poor served. Instead, the focus is on a self-fulfillment that supposedly will be attained apart from other people. Thus many American Christians understand their faith as an instrument of self-fulfillment, a way to meet private "needs."

Obviously, such an individualistic, self-centered orientation warps the Christian faith. It remolds it into a form of therapy, absorbing it into the categories of contemporary psychology. In this model, as Bellah aptly observes, "No autonomous standard of good and evil survives outside the needs of individual psyches for growth."[6]

But we are concerned with what the narrowed, individualistic conception does to a Christian view of politics. And there the effects are especially devastating.

Predictably, exaggerated individualism narrows the Christian understanding of politics. Since Americans find it difficult to imagine themselves linked in any but the most rudimentary fashion, politics is understood strictly and only as government. The way to be politically engaged is to create, adjudicate, or administer state and federal laws or directly apply pressure on those who do. For many Americans politics is at most a grubby necessity.

The vast majority of citizens think they have nothing to do with it—after all, they do not spend evenings as power brokers in smoke-filled rooms. But this is an impoverished conception of politics; it makes our politics too small.

A narrow, individualistic understanding of faith and a narrow view of politics make an unhappy combination. Their combination means that Christians concerned for the political and social health of the world bypass the church. They go directly to the only political bodies they can imagine—parties, lobbies, and governmental agencies. And in the process they put the gospel in the service of a particular political agenda. The gospel becomes strangely Republican or Democratic; it begins to sound very much like the capitalist or semisocialist line. It no longer stands in judgment of all ideologies; instead it is adapted to and serves the purposes of a single ideology.

This effect is transparent on both the religious Left and the religious Right. For the religious Left, the locus of God's activity in the world is not the church: it is socio-political liberation wherever it is occurring. For the extreme Left, the divine is active in violent revolutions aimed at freeing peoples from hunger, poverty, and oppression of any kind, from racism to sexism. The church's mission is to support (and even engage in) these revolutions. The less extreme Left reduces the church's mission to government watchdogging. The church makes its own political, social, and economic policy pronouncements and protests when government policy goes astray. Everything of any importance happening in the world happens through the channels of governmental and legislative power.

The consequence of the religious Left's perception of mission is that the church is one more political organ (and perhaps not an especially good one at that). It is divested of its uniqueness in vision and identity. To make governmental politics the whole of the church's mission is to impoverish both politics and faith.

And what about the religious Right? If the religious Left would turn the church into an agent of revolution or a lobby, the religious Right would replace the church with the nation. For it, the locus of God's activity in the world is the nation America. "God is the author of the U.S. Constitution," one politician told a gathering of fundamentalists. Since Christian America must be recovered, in one pastor's view, it is now "a sin not to be registering voters." Even spiritual revival is dependent on the nation and not the church. As another leader of the religious Right put it, "The only way to have a genuine spiritual revival is to have legislative reform. We are now, socially, so removed from a Christian consensus, that if we were to have a revival it would be short-lived."[7]

At least that leader recognizes that spiritual revival must include a social component. He realizes that individuals will not change and stay changed apart from a community that communicates and maintains that change. But an individualistic spirituality prevents him from seeing the church as just such a community. And not seeing the church, he can only look to the nation.

Both the religious Left and the religious Right, then, weaken the church's role in the world. Across the board, Christians lose a community that is uniquely Christian, explicitly based on and acting from the revelation of God in Jesus Christ. Since identity and vision are socially based, whether we know it or not, individualistic Christians of the Left or Right are especially susceptible to non-Christian influences. Because they fail to locate in and depend on a distinctive Christian community, they face the subtle assaults of the wider society with only the puny defenses of the isolated self. They are like turtles without shells, fiercely independent but utterly vulnerable to the pressures of their environment.

IN NEED OF A FAITH BOTH INDIVIDUAL AND SOCIAL

Individualistic Christianity shrinks faith and creates unhappy alliances between the church and political movements—that much we have asserted. But in so asserting we are not arguing that the church should have nothing to do with politics. The church does have a political assignment in the world. That assignment is to be a distinctive and provocative social presence. The church can only be such a presence if it attends to the story of Israel and Jesus, which gives the church its identity and vision. And it attends to its story most powerfully in its worship, the communal means of remembering its story and being shaped by it.

Faith and political effect must begin with the worshiping community because the Christian's aim is to be a particular kind of person—in the simplest terms, a person like Jesus. And every true person is both an individual and a member of a community. Personal identities and visions belong to individuals but are largely shaped by the communities to which individuals belong. We *become* personal in relation to others. We also continue to *be* personal, social, and individual creatures in relation to others. To be personal is to communicate, to care, and to do so distinctly, as only a particular person can. It is impossible to communicate and care if there are no others outside the self; it is impossible to do so distinctly if the self is not an individual. And because being a person is being individual and social, it is crucial to pay attention to the communities we grant our allegiance to. They will affect the kind of persons we become, for good or ill.

All this is a reality forgotten by individualistic Christians. It is not ignored by a more biblical Christianity. Biblical Christianity obviously includes individuals, but no less so, it includes a community, the church. The church is the faith's mediating community, the vehicle of the identity and vision God intends for his people. As Karl Barth writes, the church is "the center and medium of communication between Jesus and the world." It exists "because Jesus in His resurrection does not shatter the power of death in vain but with immediate effect; because as the witness to eternal life He cannot remain alone but at once awakens, gathers, and sends forth recipients, partners and co-witnesses of his life."[8]

To realize that faith is personal, then, is to realize that it is both individual and social. Christians are called to witness, with Christ, to God's love and power. And they are called to witness through the church, the mediating community that practices its storied faith in worship. The faith's aim is to make Christians radically different persons—persons who no longer live for self, but for God and others—and they will not be different persons merely as "isolated" individuals. They can become different only in a community that is different.

If this is so, we have found a trace of how the faith—and worship as a response to and practice of faith—inherently bears a political dimension. We need only enlarge our understanding of politics to bring this trace into the clear light of day; that is, we need to understand that politics is not exclusively governmental politics. Individual Christians serving in government are undertaking a significant work in the church's political mission. But there is more to the church's political mission, a part of the mission that includes all Christians and not only the "politicians" among them.

Before and beneath governmental politics lie the identities and worldviews of the citizenry. Even the most powerful politician cannot pursue a policy the citizens cannot imagine. Slavery, dueling, and the prohibition against women voting were all "necessary" realities that came to be seen as unnecessary—but not, at first, by those who operated the government. Another kind of politics was at work, what we call depth politics.

DEPTH POLITICS

Depth politics forms vision and identities: the way people see the world and understand their purpose in it. *Depth politics is happening whenever anyone makes a deliberate and structured attempt to influence how people live in society.*[9] Worship is a deliberate and structured attempt to influence how people, ourselves and others, live in society. So is prayer, Sunday school, or a midweek Bible study. Evangelism aims to make transformed people, people who will live differently amid other people. It is, in fact, difficult to think of an aspect of church life that does not, in one way or another, have a concern for changing the way people live—and people live in society.

This is not to politicize the church in the sense of making it simply an agent of governmental politics. It would be blasphemous to worship God in order to incite revolution or be a better Democrat. Instead, we are only recognizing that Christian worship intends to radically change the entire person—requiring, in conventional theological terms, nothing less than death and new life.

We are recognizing that the worshiping community formed on the pattern of Christ, who is "the image of the invisible God" (Col. 1:15), is necessarily a unique *polis*. Consequently, we are recognizing that to live together in conformity to that distinct pattern is to engage in depth politics. The Christian community, simply by being faithful to its worship, will inevitably and naturally be "political" (depth political). It will challenge the wider society with the truthful conception of what it means to be a person and to see the world as it really is.

As sociologist Peter Berger notes, all governmental systems depend on their constant confirmation by the citizenry. Whenever there is social transformation, "we find that the outward acts against the old order are invariably preceded by the disintegration of inward allegiances and loyalties." What Berger calls "nonrecognition and counter-definition" of a society's norms is "always potentially revolutionary."[10]

Certainly this was intuited by the Romans, who persecuted the early church. In the words of theologian Stanley Hauerwas, Christianity threatened Rome "because it was constituted by a savior who defeated the powers by revealing their true powerlessness."[11] Insurrection was not the Roman tyrant's greatest fear, since the very attempt to revolt was a compliment to his power *on its own terms.* Like the tyrant, the insurrectionist believed the world can only be changed by legal coercion and violent force and so used the same tools the tyrant did. The Roman tyrant's greater fear, then, was a community that conceived of true power in different terms, terms the tyrant could not understand or master. The church insisted that charity and humor move the world, that the last shall be first, that the servant is king, that the cross is stronger than the sword.

And what of the church in the American context, a church not facing a Roman tyrant? We need not be bent on overthrowing and destroying America to realize that the church has tremendous potency on the depth-political level. If it does not forget itself or uncritically identify with the nation or a political movement, it can present, in words and lives, "nonrecognition and counter-definition" of the social norms the rest of society accepts as immutable reality. Conversely, it can support and reinforce certain social norms that the rest of society is ready to discard.

The church, then, ideally does not seek to be either "progressive" or "conservative." It does not conceive of itself in the categories of party and governmental politics. It works to conceive of itself in the categories of the cross and to live true to those categories alone. The church is in the world so that people might learn who they are and how they can see the world by risking their lives on the revelation of God in Jesus Christ.

The church is in the world to witness to this identity and this vision as reality. Positively, it is in the world to invite the world to a joyful acceptance of this reality. Negatively, it is in the world to show the world that its "reality" is not reality, but illusion. Positively and negatively, the church engages in depth politics.

A TIME FOR TRUTH IN A DIVIDED WORLD

Perhaps it is true that the church must recover its distinctive identity and vision. Perhaps it is true that its identity and vision are conveyed in the story of Israel and Christ as celebrated in worship. Perhaps it is also true that Christians need to remember the corporate nature of their storied faith and to recognize the importance of depth politics.

All this may be true, but, practically speaking, is now a good time to practice truth? Is it realistic to expect Christians to pay new and more intense attention to the centrality of the church and its worship?

We think it is, exactly because Christians who find themselves in a divided, increasingly de-Christianized and secular society are in need. They are in need of a church, a community that does not accommodate to society's spirit and methods (as we have argued the agendas of the religious Left and Right do). Christians today need a church prepared to live by the unique truth it proclaims.

In this we find encouragement from the conclusion of George Lindbeck's important book, *The Nature of Doctrine.* Lindbeck observes that in a partly Christianized culture people assume "knowledge of a few tag ends of religious language is knowledge of the religion (although no one would make this assumption about Latin)."[12] This erroneous assumption falls away as the society in general discards the cultural marks of Christendom. Christianity is given a new slate to write on. Citizens in the surrounding society no longer presume they know the "language" that is Christianity, and Christians no longer presume their task is simply one of "translation" (which usually amounts to practical adoption of the society's non-Christian presuppositions and ways). Instead of redescribing the faith in the "foreign language" of the culture, Christians in a de-Christianized society seek to teach potential adherents the unique "language" and practices of Christianity.

In the pre-Constantinian church of the first three centuries, pagan converts did not assume they understood the grammar of faith and then decide to become Christians. Rather, as Lindbeck notes, "they were first attracted by the Christian community and form of life. . . . Only after they had acquired proficiency in the alien Christian language and form of life were they deemed able intelligently and responsibly to profess the faith, to be baptized."[13]

It appears, then, that the prospering of faith in a non-Christian cultural setting demands both a high view of the inherent truth of the gospel and a vital Christian community. Why a high view of the truth? Because where the faith is socially costly rather than convenient, it is pushed to make a claim to be "significantly different and unsurpassably true."[14] Otherwise it will hold no appeal for potential (or present) believers.

And why is community necessary? Because costly faith must show palpable signs of being true—no one will adopt it (or hold to it) on a lark—and this demands community. Any sane inquirer will look for evidences of a way of life that appears true to both the tragedy and the triumph of reality, and that enables people to negotiate life's difficult journey with honesty and grace. If Christianity evidences such a way of life, which it did to many in the ancient world, it does so in community. This is the case because ways of life are created, embodied, and passed down by communities. Just as no individual can learn and live the "American way of life" apart from the community that is the United States, no individual can learn and live the Christian way of life apart from the community that is the church.

LOOKING AHEAD

Now the base has been laid for all that will follow in succeeding chapters. We have said that the religious Left and Right apprehend that the church's purpose is to change the world, but we fear that both have not realized the fully personal (individual and social) nature of the faith and have neglected depth politics. Doing so, they have resorted to trying to change the world on the world's terms. The Left believes the church is merely political (in the sense of governmental politics) and fulfills its entire mission in being political. The Right replaces (or at least blurs) the church with the nation, but realizes that it cannot establish a theocracy.

Thus it faces the self-contradictory task of bringing the nation under Jesus Christ without ever mentioning the name of Jesus Christ.

The alternative is to let the church be the church—for it to live out the truth it celebrates in worship. We must recover, or perhaps simply pay attention to, the unique identity and vision of the church, an identity and vision shaped by the true story of God's acts in history. That story encompasses God's good creation; the despoliation of creation by the Fall; God's gracious response, initially with the nation of Israel and preeminently in the person and work of Jesus; and finally the consummation of the kingdom initiated in Christ, a consummation that draws creation out of its fallenness into its fullness. To recover the church's distinctiveness, we must learn to hear this story with an ear to its depth-political dimensions (the burden of chapters 2 through 5), and we must explore the richness of the church's untapped creativity, the dynamism of worship and service (the assignment of chapters 6 and 7).

PART TWO
THE RECOVERY OF STORY

Jesus does not seem to have had a vision of a triumphant and triumphal church encircling the globe. He always depicts for us a secret force that modifies things from within, that acts spiritually, that shows us community, unable to be anything else but community.

—Jacques Ellul, *The Subversion of Christianity*

Introduction

Few memories from boyhood are as distinct to journalist Phillip Moffitt as sitting beneath a pine tree in the Appalachian Mountains, listening to the "soft, slightly raspy voice" of his grandmother. She passed the hours telling him about living in poverty, about mountains and railroads, about his father and grandfather. Moffitt is not sure why his grandmother told him so many stories, but he is certain the stories shaped and changed him. "How can a boy act out his rage when he knows the cause of it, knows that his father and his father's father before him suffered the same rage? How can the boy's view of his parents not be inevitably altered when each week he hears more of their story, is forced to see them in the context of *their* struggle for happiness?" Listening to his grandmother's stories, the little boy learned that "all behavior was shaped by a person's history." More than that, he gained from his grandmother an understanding of his own heritage and was able to "see through her eyes without having to pay the price she had paid in living."[1]

Every individual has a story. And every society has a story. As theologian James McClendon writes, "Society may take many forms, but it *must* be narrative to be a society. The stories a people tell, the memories and traditions they share, the history they receive and modify by their own lives and pass on to their children—these are the carriers of social values."[2] Stories are crucial because they communicate to a person both an identity and a vision of the world. Narrative is uniquely equipped to convey the identity of a *person:* an individual within a society. "You can't cut characters off from their society and say much about them as individuals," writes novelist Flannery O'Connor. "You can't say anything meaningful about the mystery of personality unless you put that personality in a believable and significant social context."[3] O'Connor understands that stories uniquely mold our identities by transmitting the lifeblood of a society: "[In] the long run, a people is known, not by its statements or statistics, but by the stories it tells."[4] Stories also convey societal visions. Novelist Reynolds Price affirms that the first and final aim of story is "compulsion of belief in an order world."[5] Stories help make sense of the world; they take apparently disconnected bits and pieces and show how they fit together into a whole. The serious novelist wants the reader, through a story, to *see* the world as it is. "That—and no more, and it is everything," Joseph Conrad bluntly insists.[6]

But it is not only modern writers of fiction who find stories crucial to understanding themselves and the world. To the people of the Bible, God was known through the story of his actions in history. The Israelites knew what to do when their inquisitive children asked about God and his ways: they were to tell them the story of the Exodus. "When your son asks you in time to come, 'What is the meaning of the precepts, statutes, and laws which the Lord our God gave you?' you shall say to him, 'We were Pharaoh's slaves in Egypt, and the Lord brought us out of Egypt with his strong hand . . . " (Deut. 6:20–21). Similarly, New Testament Christians resorted to the story of Jesus to explain their startling new identity and vision. According to H. Richard Niebuhr, early preachers, "when they were hard pressed . . . turned at last to the story of their life, saying, 'What we mean is this event which happened among us and to us.' "[7]

To recover the identity and vision of the church, then, we can do better than the persons of the Bible and turn again to the story. Worship is important because it is in worship that the church enacts its story: the story of God creating a world and ordaining reality, of a world that turned against its Creator and against reality, and the story of God caring and coming to rescue the world, to restore it and make it new. It is the story of Israel, the original people of truth, and of Jesus, the victor over sin and death.

This is the story that shapes the church and forms it into a community of the kingdom, a people with the resources to live according to reality—true to the rule of God. When the church lives by its story, its presence in the world is one of political depth, a depth pointing to the world's ultimate destiny in a re-created cosmos. In the next three chapters we will consider how the story addresses evil, sin, and death; the coming of God's kingdom in Jesus; and the role of the church in a world both evil and invaded by the redemptive kingdom. We do not intend to retell the story itself but to review it and catch glimmers of both the individual and social dimensions of the faith. We will be looking for whatever sense the story may make of the depth-political aspect of our lives. We do this with the trust that now, as always, Scripture reveals the true shape of reality and will "stand in judgment on our past failures to get the whole point."[8]

2. The Politics of Evil

If the church is to be what it is supposed to be in the world, it must recover its unique identity and vision. And we have suggested what is necessary for the church to recover that true sense of itself: it must pay attention to its story, the story it enacts in worship. What does that story posit as the basis of reality, and what does it tell us about the political manifestations of evil? In a word, the story indicates that God created a world intrinsically good, but that powers of evil rose in opposition to God, intending to spoil the good creation by turning its structures of existence (institutions) into instruments of destruction.

CREATION: GOD AS THE BASIS OF REALITY

The Hebrew Scriptures begin with a confession of faith: "In the beginning God created the heavens and the earth" (Gen. 1:1, NIV). And by faith, a New Testament writer elaborates, "we perceive that the universe was fashioned by the word of God, so that the visible came forth from the invisible" (Heb. 11:3). The present age is one of acute materialism, and we moderns tend to think the visible is more real than the invisible. It is difficult for us to trust what is not directly available to the physical senses of sight, sound, touch, smell, or taste. Since the invisible God is not available to these senses, it is easy to doubt his existence.

The biblical vision of reality is exactly the opposite. Biblically, the visible, physical reality we see (or touch, taste, smell, or hear) springs from an ultimate reality that is not seen. From the strange viewpoint of the Bible, as Karl Barth writes, it makes more sense to ask "Is there a world?" than "Is there a God?" Indeed, "That there is a world is the most unheard-of thing, the miracle of the grace of God."[1] Although he is invisible, God is the measure of everything real. More than that (again speaking biblically), all that is real depends on his generosity for every moment of its existence: "all things are held together in him" (Col. 1:17).

Radically dependent on God, the universe is made to be in communion with him. And at the crown of creation stands humanity, man and woman. Man and woman are responsible to God for the well-being of the rest of creation, and in this responsibility they have a vertical relationship to God (Gen. 1:26). There is also a horizontal relationship: humanity is not complete until it is both male and female (Gen. 1:27; 5:1–2). That man and woman were created as complementary helpmeets indicates that humans are not intended to live alone.[2] People are created for a life that is individual and social, in a word, *personal*—to be lived in relation to God and other persons.

So the responsibility of human creatures in their vertical relationship to God is a social and political responsibility. Woman and man are to "rule the fish in the sea, the birds of heaven, the cattle, all wild animals on earth" (Gen. 1:26). They are placed in a garden and told to "till it and care for it" (Gen. 2:15). This is a mandate to unfold culture, to unearth nature's treasures, to build civilization and be agents of God's activity in the world.

Finally, it is clear in the scriptural story that the world and all its richness, life itself, is sheer gift. God pronounces everything he creates good (Gen. 1), signaling that all he gives in creation is intended as a sign and means of his presence, love, and communion. The world and its history is to be a drama of God's glory, the theater of his beauty. As Calvin wrote, the "sparks" of God's glory are to be seen "shining out in every individual creature."[3]

Unfortunately, the story does not end here. Instead, God's good world becomes subject to the distorting powers of evil, powers that work to move human culture away from God's will.

THE FALL AND THE INTRODUCTION OF UNREALITY

If creation by and through the generosity of God is the ground of reality, unreality and illusion are introduced at the Fall. The serpent lies; it would have humanity believe God is a despot and that men and women can be everything they should be apart from God (Gen. 3:1–6). With a political action—insurrection—Adam and Eve bring disastrous effects on individuals and societies.

First, because of the Fall people can no longer see what is real. They live in unreality and illusion and are lost in the darkness of futility (Rom. 1:20–21). Separated from God, they are at the mercy of Satan, the "father of lies" (John 8:44), and his blinding illusions (2 Cor. 4:4). In a significant sense, then, Satan's power rests in the human belief of his lies. He may accurately be defined as the "real spirit of unreality."[4] Caught up in unreality, people believe that the ultimate meaning of their existence is found in some aspect of the created order, rather than in the Creator and his will for creation. They seek meaning and salvation in sexual hedonism, materialism, a messianic American nationalism, or a communism that promises to usher in a millennium of peace and prosperity. They are now at enmity with the Creator, the basis of all reality, and at risk of his judgment (Rom. 1:18–3:19; Eph. 2:3). Integral to God's judgment is the introduction of death, a symbol of humanity's terrible separation from God, the source of all being. Fearful of judgment and death, humanity consequently is not simply blinded to reality; humanity fears reality and actively denies it.

Second, the Fall alienates person from person. It is the story of a political revolution gone awry, with chaotic results. The accursed Eve is subordinated to Adam (Gen. 3:16). Cain manifests the hostility of alienation by murdering Abel and becomes a "vagrant and wanderer on earth" (Gen. 4:1–16). Cain is a symbol of the lostness of humanity when it wanders from God, the ground of reality, and consequently finds itself not merely with a spiritual but a political and social problem. As philosopher Richard Mouw notes, "the Bible pictures hell not as the annihilation of the individual, but as a condition in which every semblance of sociality is finally eliminated and the individual is alone, weeping, wailing, and gnashing his teeth."[5]

Finally, the Fall results in the alienation of nation from nation. Babel symbolizes the breakdown in communication and understanding between separate societies (Gen. 11:1–9). With it sin and alienation have blossomed into their full political destructiveness. The history of nations—with its interminable wars, revolutions, and attempted genocides (from North American Indians to the Cambodians of Pol Pot)—is a string of bloody footnotes to the symbolic chaos of Babel. Satan is not merely the deceiver of individuals; he seduces nations (Rev. 20:3).

In summary, the Fall is a comprehensive catastrophe. The biblical story from which the church draws its vision is a story that traces evil and death back to a political act of defiance against God and reality. The original insurrection is repeated over and over again: by individuals, families, tribes, democracies, dictatorships, corporations, armies, and so on and so on, endlessly. Among the grossest offenders, of course, are the hundreds of nations that trust in their own power to control the course of history and determine its outcome. Evil, it appears, is not only individual; it is institutional and political.

THE REALITY OF THE POWERS

Though most Christians today routinely separate government and politics from religion, it is a mistake to read such a separation back into the Hebrew Scripture. The pagan nations were assigned gods by the God of Israel, Lord Most High (Deut. 32:8–9). These lesser gods (or angels), "supported, represented, and embodied the social, cultural, and political values of their societies."[6] As biblical scholar G. B. Caird notes, pagan religion and pagan political power were "inseparably associated."[7] Consequently, Israel's frequent idolatry was a religious *and* a political crime: it was Israel as a nation seeking security from a pagan god, rather than from Yahweh. The search for other gods who would protect and preserve the nation began early in Israel's history. When Moses was too long on Mount Sinai, the anxious people implored Aaron, "Come, make us gods to go ahead of us" (Exod. 32:1).

Israel's God did not consign the pagan nations to darkness and ultimate futility. True, the lesser gods turn away from God's intentions and mislead the nations (and so come to be understood as rebellious angels). But God still strives to guide all nations in the way of truth (Pss. 67:4–5; 94:10), so that all may finally worship him (Ps. 22:27; Jer. 3:17; Rev. 15:4). Israel follows God not simply for its own sake, but to be a "light to the nations" and announce salvation across the earth (Isa. 49:6). It is not unfair, then, to say that God seeks to guide individuals *and* nations to his reality and to have them live by that reality (that is, to worship the true God). The maker of heaven and earth looks forward to the day when the nations will no longer fall prey to the illusions of Satan, the real spirit of unreality (Rev. 20:3).

The presence of malevolent social influences is made even clearer in the Letters of Paul. The apostle recognizes that a host of "powers and principalities" move humanity. These include time, space, and nature (Rom. 8:38; Col. 2:8), the state (1 Cor. 2:6, 8, 12, 15:24–26; Eph. 1:20–21; Col. 1:16), and philosophy and religion (Gal. 4:1–11; Col. 2:8, 18, 20). As theologian Hendrik Berkhof writes, "Diverse human traditions, the course of earthly life as conditioned by the heavenly bodies, morality, fixed religious and ethical rules, the administration of justice and the ordering of the state—all these can be tyrants over our life."[8]

The structures that were meant to grant order and ensure a joyful peace are demonically subverted. According to the Christian story, Satan now uses putatively benevolent structures to blind humanity to reality (2 Cor. 4:4). We have lost our senses to illusion (2 Tim. 2:26) and the powers intended to serve humanity, made absolute, enslave us. Rather than trusting in the living God, societies trust in human religion, human morality, human politics, and the human mastery of nature (science). The structures of creation were intended to convey the life and love of God. Now they convey, in no small part, the death and hate of Satan.

None of these structures or institutions are evil in themselves. Societies cannot live without them. But tragically, they also cannot live with them. In the light of the Christian story, which shapes the worshiping community's vision of reality, humanity's dilemma is excruciating and could not be more desperate. Our lostness and our survival are bound up one with the other. Both depend on the lordless powers.[9]

INSTITUTIONAL EVIL

A moment's reflection on common experience is convincing: institutions of all kinds—nations, corporations, families, and yes, churches—can become beds of corruption and networks of ruin. Both the religious Right and the religious Left have recognized as much. When the Right calls attention to secular humanism and its far-reaching effects in our society's systems of government, law, and education, it is attempting to expose institutional evil. Likewise, when the left calls attention to governmental abuses of human rights, to economic systems that burden the poor, and to language that demeans women, it is attempting to expose institutional evil. Although they may disagree on its exact manifestations, both the religious Right and the religious Left acknowledge the existence of sin greater and more powerful than individuals alone.

In point of fact, isolated individuals resist the compelling, sinful tendencies of a powerful institution only rarely and heroically. Comparatively few Germans stood up against the Nazi war machine; the vast majority of Russians yield to the compulsions of the Soviet state.

Institutions are necessary and, in an important sense, good. They give human life coherence and order, and they convey the traditions of the past. But like so much else in a fallen world, institutions are not an unmixed good. Human limitations and individual sins compound in institutions and create social sin. And the compounded social sin, in turn, creates an environment that promotes individual sin.

This compounding effect explains much, yet there remains something mysterious about institutional or social sin. It is more than the simple sum of individual sins.[10] Institutions develop a life and a momentum of their own. Soon they are no longer entirely under the control of their creators. At their most sinful, as with the Third Reich, they eventually appear alien to any effective human intention and horribly destructive of all human good.

Of course, it is not necessary to live in Hitler's republic to experience the destructive effects of institutions. Institutional sin is a common, daily reality for all persons at all times. Consider the instance of families that injure their members, emotionally if not physically. The tyranny of some fathers is destructive to the entire family (the father included) and feeds on the unquestioning submission of the wife and adult children. There is a "system" of sin here that exceeds what each individual contributes to it. Similarly, the alcoholism of a single family member cannot continue unless the entire family "enables" it. The family is a manifestly good and necessary institution, yet we all know of situations in which the best (albeit tragic) counsel an individual could receive is the advice to separate from the family, to draw from a new, unpoisoned well.

The reality of institutional sin appears in families that cripple their children emotionally, in a nuclear arms race beyond human control, in job requirements that cause an individual to act against conscience, in ill-begotten laws, in misguided religious organizations. The strength of social sin is manifest anytime a conscientious person mutters, "I'm sorry, I just have to do my duty," or responsible citizens surrender with the admission that "you can't fight city hall." Like individuals, institutions embody differing degrees of sin, from minor vices to major evils. And like individuals, no institution is entirely free of sin.

THE POWERS IN THREE CONTEMPORARY INSTITUTIONS

We see that the Christian story, with its saga of the powers, provides profound resources for understanding social evil. But what does this mean for our contemporary situation? Exactly where and what powers does the church face today? There are many to choose from—sports mania, technology, various ideologies, and so on—but we have chosen to concentrate on three dominant powers: television, politicization, and consumerism.

Whether or not most Americans tend to think of *television* as an ambiguously demonic power in our society, they are agreed that it is enormously influential. E. B. White once observed a telling reaction to a lunar eclipse. When he went to the window of his Manhattan apartment to watch the eclipse, he observed all of his neighbors still at their televisions. For them, what was real was determined by the television—if the lunar eclipse had appeared there, it would have been an event even more surely than if they had seen it with their own eyes.

Both the religious Right and the religious Left have complained about television. It is commonly agreed that television purveys its own worldview focused on the recurring images of happiness through power (often violent), sensual indulgence, and material success. From soap operas to news, television mediates and legitimates a widely accepted vision of the American way of life. And it is just as commonly agreed that television is the sacramental ritual in which the entire nation partakes; TV is its own religion.[11] To note only one example: beginning with the funeral of John F. Kennedy and extending up to the explosion of the space shuttle *Challenger*, television has facilitated national ceremonies of mourning.

Perhaps because of the enormous trust placed in television, its *intrinsic* limitations are rarely recognized. Thus only its programming is protested—the religious Left, for example, typically complaining about violence in programming, the Right about sex. But to address programming alone is to fail to recognize that television is a power, that its very structure includes dimensions of destruction.

Television's ineluctable limitations mean that what is wrong with it cannot be altered merely by changing the contents of its programming. Because its technology confines it to small and indistinct images, television is intrinsically biased toward depicting what one writer calls "the grosser end of the human emotional spectrum."[12] Played out on the little screen, obvious and violent conflict makes "better" television than quiet peace; lust can be conveyed more adequately than satisfaction, the single charismatic leader better than the gradual grass-roots movement. Thus the "reality" television presents is extremely selective. Though TV would have its viewers believe it "brings the world to your door," it actually brings only oversimplified fragments of the world.

Television works wondrously at channeling simple information and entertainment. Left at that, it is nothing but a boon. But once persons invest in television the privilege not only of telling them what is new, but what is true—not only what is amusing, but what is most significant—it becomes a power separating them from God. As Malcolm Muggeridge writes, Christians are "succumbing to fantasy, of which the media are an outward and visible manifestation. Thus the effect of the media at all levels is to draw people away from reality, which means away from Christ, and into fantasy."[13]

A second contemporary manifestation of the powers is *politicization*. Politicization has no place for what we have called depth politics (the overall social involvement of persons). It allows for the politics of government alone. Taken in by the power politicization, the religious Left and Right often act as if the continuing human realities of birth, death, and lovemaking were all bound directly to the conduct of government. In truth, of course, babies are born, persons die, lovers mate, the arts, science, and much else go on in all but the most extreme political circumstances. Virginia Stem Owens rightly reminds us that when we evaluate bygone cultures we do not exclusively study their governmental systems: "We marvel, for example, at the cathedral builders and tapestry workers of medieval Europe, searching these artifacts for signs of faith and value."[14]

As with television, we can observe that governmental politics play an important and often commendable role in social life. In Jacques Ellul's words, "It is certain that politics can solve administrative problems, problems concerning the material development of a city, or general problems of economic organization—which is a considerable accomplishment."[15] But politics has its limits, and once it exceeds those limits, pretending it can provide the meaning of life or determine good and evil, it too becomes a dark power, one of the most destructive of all. Perhaps it is never more destructive than when aligned with religious zeal, whether from the side of the Right or the Left.

Finally, there is the power *consumerism.* Much of modern literature and mass media depict (and often eagerly embrace) this power. Saul Bellow renders consumerism and the chronic dissatisfaction it causes in his novel *Henderson the Rain King.* The Henderson of the title is a fifty-five-year-old, globetrotting millionaire plagued by a voice pleading, "*I want, I want.*" His desire is not satisfied with expensive projects, jaunts to Europe and Africa, or sexual promiscuity. Henderson can only confess, "My soul is like a pawn shop. . . . [I]t's filled with unredeemed pleasures, old clarinets, and cameras, and moth-eaten fur."[16]

Though perhaps not as intensely as Henderson, all of us hear the nagging voice of consumerism. Speaking of consumption, the economist John Kenneth Galbraith asserts that "on no other matter, religious, political, or moral," is the individual so "elaborately and skillfully and expensively instructed."[17] And as E. F. Schumacher, Henry Fairlie, George F. Will, and other commentators of all political and economic stripes have noted, consumerism runs directly counter to the grain of traditional Christianity. Consumerism promotes instantaneous "fulfillment" by indulgence; Christianity considers fulfillment to be part of an ongoing struggle, perfected in the end only as sheer gift. Consumerism would have the ideal person focused on self and its "needs"; Christianity turns the person outward to the genuine needs of others.

As with television and governmental politics, we can observe that consumption, within limits, is good. It is necessary and good that people not be hungry or thirsty; it is good to have a warm home and enough possessions to celebrate family and friendship. But once again the power breaks through its rightful boundaries: consumerism, rather than a path of life, is a treadmill of death, spinning ever faster as our frantic needs grow more gluttonous. And as with the other powers, Christians succumb to its illusions, thinking Jesus must be sold like soap, that a people following the homeless son of a carpenter cannot be what it should be without banks full of wealth. Said one television evangelist, "The church won't be able to do much if [the world] can keep it poor and under-financed. The billion dollar category is what is needed to be truly effective."[18]

In summary, we can note four features common to each of these contemporary powers. First, each is good within its proper limits but becomes diabolical when it expands beyond those limits. Second, each pretends to encompass and determine basic reality and so is directly in conflict with the claims of the Christian story. Third, pretending to be the key to reality in its fullness, each wants to be judged only on its own criteria. As a consequence, each will attempt to re-create Christianity in its own image. (Thus consumerism, for example, would make the radical gift of grace into a commodity that, once possessed, will guarantee health and wealth.) And fourth, each of the powers is not what it appears to be—even in its outlaw proportions, it seems benevolent and utterly necessary for humanity to continue a supposedly full life, but in reality the power is destructive and inimical to an authentically rich life.

THE IMPACT OF THE POWERS ON THE PERSON

A human being becomes personal and continues to be personal in relation to others. Since the powers affect individuals and society, we can intensify our awareness of the powers by exploring how they influence the person: an individual within society. Briefly put, they do so by acting on the individual's identity and vision. They operate principally on a depth-political level, ordering and forming social structures.

The powers mold *identity* by suggesting (to use a mild term) what roles persons should adopt in society. The powers tell persons how they should fundamentally understand themselves and what factors will help to determine their "true" worth. Consumerism, for example, insists that human beings are essentially consumers. A person's level of acquisition is an indicator of her value in the world.

The power politicization, on the other hand, would have persons believe they are preeminently political animals and that they are not doing anything worthwhile if they are not somehow involved with government. In such an atmosphere, as Jacques Ellul writes, "A poet restricting himself to being a poet without signing petitions or manifestos would immediately be accused of retiring to his ivory tower."[19]

We observe, then, that the powers present persons with roles that will determine their identities. Each of these roles implies a corresponding list of virtues and vices. For television, it is a vice to be homely, quiet spoken, and unostentatious. For consumerism, it is a vice to cultivate thrift or spurn luxury.

The aspect of the powers that forms social identities has many ramifications. But not the least is the fact that the conversion of any one individual will not, by itself, change the identity-forming influence of the powers. As James McClendon notes, "it is vital *not* to imagine that when some rulers become church members, the conversion of the great power over which those rulers preside has already taken place."[20] Likewise, as we have noted, television will not change simply because church members buy and operate a network. To truly engage the powers, we must look instead to an *entire community* of converted persons committed to rejecting the individual and social identity granted by the powers and to defining its identity instead by the story of Jesus. The fallacy of the social endeavors of the religious Left and Right is that they overlook the centrality of exactly such a community.

The powers also present persons with their own *visions.* They put forth their own gods, demanding their own kinds of absolute allegiance. Politicization, for example, holds forth the state. Consumerism makes a god of Mammon. In all cases the powers tell people their own stories about the purpose of life and what is good or evil. By accepting one power or another, persons accept its declaration of the "true" end of life, of what they should strive to be and do. If politicization is the ultimate power, the presidency or a seat in Congress will loom as the highest goal of existence. If television is the dominant power, persons in its thrall will imagine nothing more exhilarating than fame, even if it lasts only fifteen minutes.

In all their furious multitude, the powers are enormously dominant, leading individuals and societies astray day by day. Yet penetrating and hiding within the vital structures of our existence, the powers seem not to appear. They are the "hidden wirepullers in man's great and small enterprises, movements, achievements, and revolutions."[21]

Thus the powers breed confusion on every side, confounding a society's vision or worldview by appearing in one form or another, then never seeming to appear at all. As the British pastor Kenneth Leech observes, "Idolatry is closely linked with loss of vision."[22] The biblical prophets were able to speak for God to Israel because they regained a vision of what is real, beyond the illusions of the powers. Amos and Isaiah spoke after potent occurrences of such vision (see Amos 1:1; Isa. 1:1). Joel awaited the day when all people would see with the vision of the prophets, basing their worldview on the lordship of God alone (Joel 2:27–28). Since our vision is something both individual and social, it, like identity, makes community a necessity. Is there a community wherein, as Joel expected, the sons and daughters prophesy, witnessing at last faint glimmers of what is truly real?

Obviously we believe there is. The church is a community with a story that gives it vision to see through the false dominance of all powers, political included. The work of the church in the world is not to be understood in terms of the political agendas of any movements or nations. Instead, the church's work is to be understood on its own terms, borne in its own story: the terms of the cross and resurrection.

IN SUMMARY: INDIVIDUAL AND SOCIAL SIN

We began this chapter with a two-part question: what does the biblical story celebrated in worship tell us about the basis of reality and about the manifestations of evil on a depth-political level? We have found that, from beginning to end, the Christian story recognizes the presence of profound evil. Sin damaged and damages all creation; and it affects the person in both aspects, individual and social. It manifests itself in the structures of existence that were intended to channel the lifegiving presence of God, warping those structures or powers into malignant barriers between God and humanity. These powers are not found only in spectacularly evil and distant lands, such as Pol Pot's Cambodia or Stalin's Russia. They hold sway over the entire earth, enslaving all nations, and may do so in supposedly innocuous forms such as television or consumerism. Thus they are most frequently found not in governmental politics, but depth politics.

The powers move humanity by force of the false identities and visions they press on persons. According to the Christian story, God is ultimate reality, but persons are blinded both in what they do (identity) and in what they see and will be (vision). Since the powers are embedded in social structures, we cannot pretend that either individual conversions alone or alterations in the structures alone will result in a full and true redemption or restoration of the creation. The converted individual, apart from any converted structure, will face enormous pressure to conform to the whims of the powers. Even the heroic person will find herself directly participating in the injustice and immorality of the wider society. Conversely, an altered social structure will not be free from the sinful impulses of the individuals who alter it and those who later maintain it. It may be corrected in respect to one abuse, only later to perpetuate (after the designs of a competing power?) a dozen other abuses.

Of course, no one who knows the Christian story expects a perfected world short of the consummation of God's kingdom. But that brings us to our next step, the subject of the chapter to come. Exactly how did Jesus confront the powers, and what meaning has his life and death for modern Christians who realize they must engage the powers on a depth-political level? In worship Christians confess that the life and death of Jesus have made a world-changing difference, even short of the consummation. Our contention at this point can be simply stated: Christ cannot be said to have made *any* difference in the lives of individuals or societies unless he has made a real difference in both.

3. Jesus and Depth Politics

In *Pilgrim at Tinker Creek,* Annie Dillard describes the early aftermath of the discovery of safe cataract surgery. Surgeons ranged across America and Europe operating on dozens of men and women who had been blind since birth. For the first time in their lives, these patients saw light, the stars, a lover's face.

But their new sight was not experienced as pure joy. For those who had never seen, seeing was a demanding task. They had to learn to distinguish objects, to make sense of the confusions of motion, to understand space not by touch or sound, but by sight. Many went so far as to refuse the gift of this new sense. A child apathetically refused to look at objects more than a foot away. A young woman shut her eyes and proceeded about the house in her old, familiar fashion. A teenage boy finally blurted, "No, really, I can't stand it any more. . . . If things aren't altered, I'll tear my eyes out."[1]

THE CHALLENGE OF JESUS' LIFE AND DEATH

As common sense would have it, any blind person would naturally want to see, and any sane person would want to be delivered from the grip of sin and death. But as we noted in the previous chapter, the Christian story affirms that humanity is blind and does not want to see. Like those who have grown accustomed to physical darkness, humanity actually prefers to keep its own sort of blindness in relation to God, the base of reality.

And it is dismaying to witness this tendency even among those who believe the good news of Jesus Christ and are now supposed to see. The church's great temptation is to make the good news easy by adapting it to systems and ideologies that are already congenial and demand little sacrifice, little difference with the world. We sometimes see this convenient adaptation in the religious Right, when the gospel is reduced to a message of private peace of mind, docile and uncritical citizenship, material prosperity, and uninterrupted health. Jesus, it appears, must have been an upper-middle-class, patriotic, Republican businessman.

And we sometimes see the same kind of adaptation in the religious Left. Here the gospel is reduced to a message of centralized government, unending federal programs, an ever-growing list of individual "rights," and freedom from all constrictions on the personal pursuit of happiness. From this angle, Jesus appears to have been an urbane, fashionably detached, self-centered member of what has been called the New Class—professors, journalists, bureaucrats, and other manipulators of words and ideas.

In the end, neither of these visions is so different from what the blinded world offers: they are only more of it. Their diluted gospels are, in some ways, a darker blindness, what Kierkegaard scorned as "a heedless reverence for him whom one must either believe in or be offended at."[2]

What we miss, if such is our gospel, is the sheer, sometimes frightening creativity of Jesus' life and message. In a way, American Christians know Jesus too well. His parables are like old jokes to them—the tired punchlines are memorized, so why hear them again? His deeds, especially his death on a cross, have been dogmatized for centuries and, though still called mysterious, ostensibly have all their meaning explained.

But in first-century Palestine there was no such attitude. The parables were baffling and astonishing. The deeds were shocking. Who was Jesus the Nazarene? God and the demons knew him as the Son of God; his family considered him crazy; the authorities viewed him as a criminal, a blasphemer, and a soldier of Satan; the crowds saw him as John the Baptist raised, or Elijah, or another prophet; and the disciples finally identified him as the anointed one, but did not grasp what that meant until after his death.

In this chapter we want to take up the central episode of the Christian story, to consider again who this man Jesus' was. Our special aim is to explore what political relevance Jesus' ministry, death, and resurrection had—and have. We will not contend that Jesus had a political program in the same way a presidential candidate has a platform. But we will contend that Jesus had a political posture, a posture intended to reveal God's intentions for society.[3] Jesus' death and resurrection have political significance. He was not a politician in the ordinary sense of the word, yet he confronted the powers, inaugurated a kingdom with individual, social, and even cosmic ramifications, and taught (especially in his parables) a people of the truth how to live. In all this he was the consummate depth politician.

CHRIST'S CONFRONTATION OF THE POWERS

As Paul declared in the earliest days of the faith, the cross is central to the life and ministry of Jesus (1 Cor. 1:17; 15:3–19). Each of the four Gospels build toward and climax at the cross, devoting a disproportionate amount of its pages to those three fateful days in Jerusalem. If the work of the cross has no depth-political dimension, it is incredible to think that Jesus was vitally concerned with that dimension.

In fact, the cross was the ultimate depth-political event, for on the cross Jesus confronted and defeated the powers. It is the powers, as we have noted, that move societies at the depth-political level. They provide identities and visions believed to stave off chaos, meaninglessness—and death.

It is death, after all, that humanity fears most. In his illuminating book *The Denial of Death*, Ernest Becker argues that the fear of death is "the basic fear that influences all others."[4] He reminds his readers that the mystery cults of the eastern Mediterranean were attempts to gain immunity "from the greatest evil: death and the dread of it."[5] Indeed, all religions address the paramount problem of how to bear the end of life, and Schopenhauer called death the real "muse of philosophy."[6]

Death is a primal and inescapable reality that moves societies as surely as it does individuals. It threatens all that we know and do. What is worthwhile to do or be if nothing will last, if one's work of art will simply rot and one's lover will eventually decay and feed worms? The sting of death underlies the potency of the principalities and powers. Faced with the threat of extinction, individuals are prone to flee to the societal constants that existed before they were born and will continue to exist long after they are gone. There must be something individuals can devote their lives to, gaining the assurance that their existence has significance. In Becker's words,

All of us are driven to be supported in a self-forgetful way, ignorant of what energies we really draw on, of the kind of lie we have fashioned in order to live securely and serenely. Augustine was a master analyst of this, as were Kierkegaard, Scheler, and Tillich in our day. They saw man could strut and boast all he wanted, but that he really drew his 'courage to be' from a god, a string of sexual conquests, a Big Brother, a flag, a proletariat, and the fetish of money and the size of a bank balance.[7]

The fear of death is so great that men and women will live in enslavement and deny reality in an attempt to overcome or repress it.

Yet the confession of faith is that death has lost its sting (1 Cor. 15:55). Death attempted to own Jesus, to reduce to insignificance he who finally hung on a humiliating cross between two criminals. Jesus, however, had never given in to sin, and so death had no power over him: it swallowed him—his death was a real and total death, bleaker and lonelier than any other man's—but it could not contain him, and in its apparent moment of highest triumph death was shattered. And with it was shattered the strength of the powers, since death was their ultimate leverage, the instrument always at hand to reduce individuals and societies to timidity and compliance.

On the cross Jesus disarmed the powers and exposed the falsity of their pretensions. He "made a public spectacle of them" (Col. 2:15, NIV), exposing the illusion of their claims to lend immortality and significance to human lives. His resurrection is validation that death is overcome. In place of the illusion of the powers is put the reality that "neither death nor life, . . . nor any powers, . . . will be able to separate us from the love of God that is in Jesus Christ our Lord" (Rom. 8:38– 39, NIV).

The cross is a sign that no power is absolute, however terrifying it may be, however large the numbers of people who leap to do its bidding. The cross is the charge that sinks beneath any single individual's reality and explodes at the deepest of depth-political levels. The explosion hurls outward from the cross-center with a force that supplants any and every corrupt social structure that pretends to be absolute. In crucifying Christ the powers were not "gaining control over Christ but losing control over all men."[8] It is from the cross that Jesus reigns, Lord and sustainer of creation, drawing all to himself and deserving ultimate allegiance (John 12:32; Col. 1:17).

His death is a criticism of the dominant human tendency to turn to the powers (against him) because they grant us the illusion that we can control our lives. Through a failure of vision we depend on the false reign of the powers. Like the overly dependent (adult) child who realizes he would be better off if he gained independence from his parents, we sometimes know we should break free of the powers. But (again like the adult child), we are afraid of losing our identity and vision if we leave our familiar resources—those powers that define social roles and apparently lend the world meaning.

Even when we wish for better, then, we are frozen by insecurity. Yet the cross stands as a sign that there is life after the powers, that we can live "out of control," confident that an identity and vision grounded in the Jesus story will be sustained by God's gracious surprises.[9]

Thus the cross calls us away from the fraudulent safety of powers-induced, self-centered individualism. Jesus expects his followers to begin living according to the pattern of the cross and stop living according to the pattern of the powers. The powers turn us in on self; they assure us we must "look out for number one." The cross, on the other hand, is "the demand for a new quality of life," a quality of life not "centered on personal ambitions and indifferent to the needs of others," but characterized by love and service.[10] This is the social agenda of the cross. It is the depth politics of Jesus.

THE KINGDOM OF GOD: INDIVIDUAL AND SOCIAL

The vision the cross gives us is not solely political, but it certainly includes politics, for sin and death, with all their social ramifications, are defeated. The powers may still rage, but their doom is sealed. The Christian story looks ahead to a new heaven and a new earth, a creation in which individuals will be at peace (Rev. 21:4) and nations will no longer go to war (Mic. 4:3).

This is an eschatological vision, one that sees the end and goal of history. But the eschatological vision is not concerned merely with the future, for in Jesus the future has invaded the present. The kingdom of God has begun. It was not only at the cross that Jesus had a social agenda.

New Testament scholars are agreed that the kingdom, the "dynamic concept of the rule of God," was the "heart of [Jesus'] proclamation and the key to his entire mission."[11] He began his ministry with a pronouncement: "The time has come; the kingdom of God is upon you; repent, and believe the gospel" (Mark 1:15).

Certainly this kingdom affected individuals. Jesus' call to repentance was aimed at individuals, and he frequently challenged persons apart from the crowd: the disciples in Galilee, called in pairs away from their fishing nets; Nicodemus, who came in the night; or the lone centurion. Ultimately each individual decided for or against Jesus, and if he or she decided for him, that person was no longer considered an enemy of God. By trusting and obeying Jesus each man or woman found his or her true self (Matt. 16:24–25) and received eternal life (John 3:16–17). God's love and forgiveness, to be known by the individual, are indisputably essential to the kingdom Jesus announced.

Yet the kingdom also had political overtones. The angels proclaimed "peace *among* men" at the nativity (Luke 2:14, RSV), and Jesus disturbed the political authorities from his birth (Herod in Matt. 2) to his death-turned-resurrection (see Matt. 28:11–15).

Significantly, the language used to describe Jesus and his mission was thoroughly political. "Kingdom" itself was a term borrowed from politics. "Gospel" was used within the cult of the Roman emperor to refer to the announcement of the birth of an heir to a throne, an heir's coming of age, or his accession to the throne. Even "Christ" was a political title: "one anointed to rule."[12] We should not be too quick to dismiss these descriptions as "only" metaphors, emptying them of any political content. As the Latin American evangelical theologian C. Rene Padilla affirms, Jesus' "kingdom is not of this world—not in the sense that it has nothing to do with the world, but in the sense that it does not adapt itself to human politics. It is a kingdom with its own politics, marked by sacrifice."[13] Jesus inaugurated a kingdom that affected both individuals and societies—persons in their fullness. As we saw in the previous chapter, sin is not merely individual; the powers strive to hold sway over society as well. Accordingly, the kingdom confronts evil in every one of its dimensions. In all his words and deeds, we witness the double-edged sword of Jesus' ministry piercing individuals *and* society.

The church is in the world to live by the mandates of Jesus' kingdom, not the mandates of nations, revolutionaries, or any other powers. Therefore an understanding of that kingdom and its contours is crucial. What kind of people would the kingdom have us be? We turn again to the story of Jesus, the inaugurator of the kingdom.

THE KINGDOM AND THE PARABLES

Even as there are established political options championed by religious leaders in our day, there were established political options in Jesus' day: the accommodation of Sadduceeism and Pharisaism, the violent rebellion proposed by the Zealots, and the mystical withdrawal of the Essenes. In its own eyes, the public at large could (at best) hope for a military messiah to lead Israel to victory over the occupying Romans and to a reign of prosperity. Even those closest to Jesus, halfway through his ministry, hoped to sit in privileged positions beside his earthly throne (Mark 10:35–37).

And yet it was obvious to Jesus' listeners by his consternation and unsettling statements that the meaning of the kingdom he had in mind escaped them, so they continually queried him about its nature. His baffling replies were not the kind of help they desired. The replies were often riddles, parables that seemed to reverse fundamental expectations about the Roman-routing kingdom his followers so eagerly awaited. We can justifiably suspect the response of these followers is fairly described by a modern scholar: "I don't know what you mean by that story but I'm certain I don't like it."[14]

Jesus' followers thought the kingdom would be transparently mighty and glorious. If it was to be compared to a plant, then surely the towering cedar of Lebanon was appropriate. The prophet, after all, was told to compare the strength and majesty of Egypt to the cedar, standing taller than all other trees, with branches that "overshadowed the forest." In its boughs "all the birds of the air had their nests" (Ezek. 31:3–6). The same figure was used for Nebuchadnezzar, king of Babylon. The tree's top touched the sky, and "the birds lodged in its branches" (Dan. 4:10–12).

These were the botanical metaphors of power Jesus' listeners had heard from birth. And yet when he came explicitly declaring the kingdom of God, he compared it to the mustard tree. "What is the kingdom of God like? . . . It is like a mustard seed which a man took and sowed in his garden; and it grew to be a tree and the birds came to roost among its branches" (Luke 13:18–19). Using language so similar to that of the familiar prophecies ("the birds came to roost among its branches"), Jesus apparently was intentionally reversing the kingdom expectations of his followers. They hoped for a kingdom as patently commanding as the cloud-piercing cedar of Lebanon, but Jesus likened the true kingdom to the lowly mustard tree, little more than a shrub.

The parable of the good Samaritan (Luke 10) was hardly less surprising. As if it were not enough that the parable had the supposedly respectable persons (the priest and Levite) doing nothing to aid the wounded man, it was one of a despised people (the Samaritans; see John 4:9) stopping to lend exemplary assistance. Perhaps a comparable shock could be elicited in today's terms if we spoke of the pope or the president of the United States blithely walking by an injured man, only to have one of Khadaffy's terrorists happen on the scene, gently lift the wounded man to his feet, and carry him to the nearest hospital. As John Dominic Crossan writes, whatever else the parable means, it is "an attack on the structure of expectation."[15] If Jesus' listeners thought they understood exactly what it meant to live under God's rule, they could only have been scratching their heads after such a tale, worried at the sinking feeling in their stomachs.

The examples could be multiplied, for Jesus often spoke in puzzling parables. Laborers are paid the same regardless of the hours each spent at work; a feast is served to strangers and friends are turned away; the wasteful, selfish younger son returns home and gets the party his responsible elder brother never had; the immoral tax collector's prayers are heard, but not those of the clergyman.

The riddles of Jesus were about individuals, but they also cause his hearers to wonder anew about social groups. Does the kingdom depend on what this world calls power? What about tax collectors and Samaritans? Are they entirely evil? And priests and lawyers—are they always right? Instead of reinforcing the comfortable preconceptions of the pious, the parables, wrought with considerable artistry, "give God room." As Crossan puts it, "They remove our defenses and make us vulnerable to God. It is only in such experiences that God can touch us, and only in such moments does the kingdom of God arrive."[16]

THE KINGDOM AND THE CONFRONTATION WITH SATAN

According to the Gospels of Matthew, Mark, and Luke, Jesus directly confronted Satan at the beginning of his ministry. The devil tempted Jesus with bread, political authority, and exploitation of God's protection. The Son of God resisted on all three counts and emerged from the desert proclaiming the kingdom of God. In a sense, after this direct encounter he had already defeated the power of darkness.[17] It was clear that Jesus was stronger than Satan; the outcome of every future struggle between Jesus and Satan was predetermined.

The subsequent exorcisms prove no less. The demons shriek in terror when Jesus approaches, immediately identifying him as the "Holy One of God" (Mark 1:24). Exorcists were not unusual in New Testament times, but Jesus' swift dispatch of the demons revealed an extraordinary authority (Mark 1:27). Other exorcists commonly bargained with demons, performed elaborate rituals, or conjured up an opposing demon and pitted it against the demon in control of the possessed. Jesus merely commanded the unclean spirits to depart, reducing them to fearful submission with a word.

The temptation and subsequent exorcisms depict Jesus confronting evil at its root. Jesus, as an individual, is faced with the temptations of evil, and evil possesses other individuals who are rescued by Jesus' exorcisms. At the same time, he does not ignore evil in its social manifestations. Satan, after all, tempts Jesus with political authority. This indicates that political authority is Satan's to give and betrays the possibility of demonic presence in social systems. Here as elsewhere, "evil is implicitly recognized to have a societal character."[18]

THE KINGDOM AND THE GENTILES

For a Jew in Jesus' day, it was one thing to suggest redemption would include the physical world; it was another thing entirely to suggest Gentiles would enter the kingdom. Yet this is exactly what

Jesus did. He rebuked negative attitudes toward Samaritans (Luke 9:51–56). More, he used these hated neighbors as examples to put Israelites to shame (Luke 10:25–37; 17:18). He openly expected Ninevites, the Queen of Sheba, and even those of Sodom and Gomorrah to surpass some Israelites at the advent of God's judgment (Matt. 12:41–42; Matt. 10:15). "Many," he said, "will come from east and west to feast with Abraham, Isaac, and Jacob in the Kingdom of Heaven" (Matt. 8:11).

Hatred separated individual Jews and Gentiles, but so did deeply ingrained traditions and customs. Jesus opened the kingdom to Gentiles, thereby attacking a massive social barrier and suggesting, in this way as with others, that the kingdom is God's healing rule over humanity, both individual and social.

THE KINGDOM AND THE ABSOLUTE PRIORITY OF THE FAMILY

In addressing Jesus' inclusion of Gentiles in the kingdom we have seen just how fundamentally he confronted both individuals and social structures. But there was another institution more basic to the social structure of Israel than its tense relation to Gentile neighbors: family ties and roles. Even these were not left untouched by the kingdom Jesus introduced.

His own family once asked to see him, but he pointed to his disciples and said, "Here are my mothers and my brothers. Whoever does the will of my heavenly Father is my brother, my sister, my mother" (Matt. 12:49–50). The disciples left families to follow Jesus (Mark 10:28–31), and it is in reference to families split asunder that Jesus warned, "You must not think I have come to bring peace on earth" (Matt. 10:34–36).

In this respect, Jesus' ministry was no less disturbing than the effects of modern "cults" who call their members away from kin. Of course there is no basis for assuming Jesus wanted to abolish the family. But his actions and teachings indicate that even this most meaningful and fulfilling of human institutions cannot be absolute. The work of the kingdom may call spouse or son or daughter away from family; to this day a serious confession of faith can throw families into conflict. No institution molds or shapes individuals as profoundly as the family; no society exists without families. Few principalities or powers can be more benevolent *or* more destructive than the family. And in the work of Christ this power, too, is brought under the rule of God.

THE KINGDOM AND PARENTHETICAL PEOPLE

Of all Jesus' actions, few were so creative or so controversial as his unstinting compassion for the forgotten people of this world—the poor and the outcast, and women and children, all of whom dwelled in the shadows of society. We could say these were the persons society put in parentheses, making them optional, dispensable, unimportant. Yet the kingdom come in Jesus revealed that the society knew a flawed grammar: the persons made parenthetical were not dispensable at all—Jesus put exclamation points after them to call attention to their true importance.

As Luke's Gospel recognizes most sharply, Jesus came among the poor and especially to the poor. Mary's Magnificat rejoices that the hungry and poor will be exalted (Luke 1:46–55); the "Sermon on the Plain" blesses the poor (Luke 6:20–26); and several parables warn the rich while succoring the poor (Luke 12:13–21; 14:12–24; 16:19–31).

Dining with the outcasts was an enactment of Jesus' parables. With this action Jesus *embodied* the parables, putting flesh and blood behind what he had spoken. With it he both offered hope of salvation to those told they were beyond hope and threatened the careful social distinctions of his time. In his spoken parables he suggested God heard the prayer of a lowly tax collector; in his enacted parables he sat down to table and shared food with the tax collector. It was bold enough to criticize with words. Jesus' audacious action hinted that the "wrong" were as entitled to God's mercy as the "right" and revealed that Jesus was in dead earnest when he said as much.

Barely less startling was Jesus' attitude toward women. He lived in a society where women could be divorced because they were not pretty, failed to bear children, or were simply poor cooks. Property was held mostly by men. A woman's testimony was not accepted in court, and no self-respecting rabbi would take women as disciples. A popular rabbinic saying summarized the status of the sexes well: "Praised be God that he has not created me a Gentile; praised be God that he has not created me a woman."

It was in this atmosphere that Jesus, telling a parable, used a woman to represent God (Luke 15:8–10). In many quarters women dared not speak to a man in public; Jesus conversed with women at length (Matt. 15:21–28; Mark 5:25–34; Luke 7:36–50). Women were primarily domestic servants, yet Jesus reproved Martha for her scrupulous service and affirmed Mary, who, contrary to custom, was absorbing his teaching (Luke 10:38–42; see also John 4). He explicitly rejected the notion that a woman's worth came through childbearing, predicating it instead on hearing and obeying God (Luke 11:27–28). Contemporary laws viewed a wife's adultery more seriously than a husband's, but Jesus placed them on the same plane—which was enough to make the (male) disciples wonder if marriage was worth the trouble (Matt. 19:9–10; see also Mark 10:10–12).[19]

Once again we may remark on both the individual and social dimensions of Jesus' life. He teaches, heals, and offers God's deliverance to women as worthy and responsible individuals, and does it in such a way that the social expectations of that sex are jarred and tipped bottom side up. What could it mean that one who spoke and acted with such authority treated women more respectfully than did those who possessed a less impressive authority?

Removed from the customs of Jesus' culture, we are likely to miss another aspect of his radical willingness to run against the grain of dominant social customs. Children, like women, occupied a precarious societal position in that day. Infanticide was a family right in Greek and Roman cultures; in the later Hellenistic period daughters were usually discarded and, when kept, were seen more or less as pets. Children were regularly sold into concubinage, with boy brothels dotting most Mediterranean cities.

In Hebrew society children, like women, were considered members of the people of God by virtue of their association with the adult males in the family. Children were among society's parenthetical people and ordinarily ignored in public, so that one "would have to search long and hard . . . to find any benevolence toward the young comparable to Jesus' embracing and blessing of children."[20] Jesus commended children's dependence and openness to wonder (Mark 9:35–37; Matt. 18:1–6; 19:13–15). It was individual children that Jesus touched and spoke to; it was children in general—a social group—that benefited from his elevated estimate of the child's worth.

Jesus' constant attention to the parenthetical people of his time—the poor, the outcast, women, and children—is one of the most remarkable aspects of his ministry. It was not that the parenthetical people were so exemplary that they stood above the need for repentance. Indeed, Christ called these people "sinners," in need of God's forgiveness no less than the rich and powerful (Luke 5:32). Clearly, the demand for repentance and invitation to salvation is aimed at individuals, not a particular social class, and cannot be reduced to a political program. Conservative Christians are justified when they insist that there is no kingdom or even the hint of the kingdom if it excludes personal reconciliation with the God revealed in Jesus Christ.

At the same time, as more liberal Christians emphasize, the kingdom in its fullness includes an acute social concern. The Christian story will not allow otherwise. It is the parenthetical people who behave in a manner Jesus judges most suitable to the kingdom. He commends the poor widow for giving all she has. He praises a woman who anoints him with oil worth a year's salary. He tells the disciples not to emulate the wealthy man who will not sell his goods and presents children and slaves as examples of discipleship. It is not that the parenthetical people are perfect or possess some intrinsic merit. But perhaps exactly because they have nothing to lose, they are willing to admit their need and to live in openness to the surprises of God's kingdom.

Those surprises are sometimes—often—critical, and Jesus' compassion is a courageous and potent form of social criticism. It is a full-bodied compassion, demanding repentance and reconciliation with God of the poor just as surely as it demands the same of the rich. But it is a compassion that does not side with the powerful who so eagerly want to restrict God's love to the private, "spiritual" realm, preserving a social arrangement advantageous to their interests. Jesus' compassion admits the hurt of society's parenthetical people, refusing to accept their pain as normal or natural. Accepting it is the way of ordinary human, social inertia.

The powers, now as then, would have Christians believe there is no other way: this society, this administration, this economic program is the best that can be.

These powers are apt to promote sentimental charity—the donation of a few dollars to soothe the private conscience—while leaving the social system exactly as it was. Such charity can be a tactic to keep the real pain of the disadvantaged out of sight and out of mind, to keep the parenthetical people parenthetical. It fits an attitude of "official optimism," the steady insistence by government, commerce, and popular culture that all is well and only getting better. Jesus' compassion, however, is not sentimental or cheap. It admits the pain of the parenthetical people and passionately opposes any "official optimism" that ignores, downplays, or denies human tragedy in its midst.

"Quite clearly," Walter Brueggemann writes, "the one thing the dominant culture cannot tolerate or co-opt is compassion, the ability to stand in solidarity with the victims of the present order. It can manage charity and good intentions, but it has no way to resist solidarity with pain or grief."[21] Jesus, the unexcelled depth politician, stood in answering solidarity with the pain and grief suffered by the parenthetical people of his day.

THE KINGDOM AND FORGIVENESS OF SIN

We turn finally to Jesus' forgiveness of sin, which, characteristically, was stunningly bold. The action excited accusations of blasphemy (Mark 2:7) and marked Jesus as someone claiming a religiously and politically dangerous level of authority. On this count we see just how tightly the individual and the social were bound together in the work of Jesus.

Clearly, the forgiveness of sin concerned individuals. This deed of Jesus' does not fit neatly into the scheme of those who would reduce Christianity to a political program, revolution on behalf of the poor. After all, it is most often exactly the poor, the outcast, and the sick who are offered forgiveness by Jesus (see Matt. 9:1–9; Luke 7:36–50). The forgiveness he offers is not the promise of acceptance by human society—that would prompt no charges of blasphemy. He grants the acceptance of God himself.

Yet even this most intimate of Jesus' actions is not without its social dimension. As Walter Brueggemann reminds us, the managers of society presume to determine and punish sin (with ostracism if nothing else). Those who control the social "apparatus for forgiveness" thus wield tremendous control. Consequently, Jesus' forgiveness of sin was both religiously staggering and a breathtaking threat to the accepted forms of social control.[22] It showed that what mattered most to persons—their acceptability before God—could not be regulated by those who ran society. Freed of ultimate condemnation—rejection by God—who need fear so much the condemnation of any human government or religious organization? Jesus' forgiveness was socially empowering.

IN SUMMARY: THE KINGDOM AND THE POWERS

We have briefly surveyed the salient aspects of Jesus' ministry, attempting to delineate how the cross and the kingdom he announced fundamentally confront individuals and societies, working dramatically at the level of depth politics. Perhaps it will now be wise to summarize our understanding of God's rule and his victory, through Christ, over the powers.

The kingdom has begun. Jesus came announcing it and calling on his bearers to repent. The kingdom is God's rule, his power made visible through concrete signs—healed bodies, routed demons, and so on—that point to Jesus as the Messiah. The kingdom has entered private and public history, affecting human life in all of its dimensions, socially no less than individually. As Allen Verhey comments, the kingdom "may not be reduced to political dispositions and behavior, but it clearly includes them."[23]

Yet if God's kingdom has come, it has obviously not come in its completeness. Every dimension of human experience remains profoundly affected by sin and evil. The consummation or perfection of the kingdom lies somewhere in the unknown future, and it will come entirely by God's power, as his gift. Until then, the church lives eschatologically, in a tension between the future and the present. It lives now in the reality of the age to come. The old age continues, but the new age has begun; the new order is hidden in the old; there is a "present fulfillment in the setting of future consummation."[24]

Satan and the powers have been dealt the decisive blow. The

real spirit of unreality remains but has been definitively exposed by Jesus' ministry and the cross. The powerful institutions of Jesus' day (and, by extension, those of our day) were confronted and unmasked as less than absolute. Jesus obviously drew from the traditions and institutions of his day, but he considered none beyond criticism or the need of reform.

If, as Dorothy Sayers submits, life is not so much a problem to be solved as a medium for creation, Jesus was the consummate artist.[25] Working resourcefully with the stuff of his culture, he crafted nothing less than a new world. He used stories, pithy and colorful teaching, and bold, sweeping gestures (enacted parables) to communicate the full richness of the kingdom, which has certainly come, though its perfection awaits. Even his death, ugly and desperate as it was, was something shaped to his own purposes, an instrument of individual and social redemption.

In Jesus' ministry we observe none of the awkward dichotomies that plague Christian mission today. Some Christians major in social action but often neglect evangelism. And others are vigilant about evangelizing individuals but are reluctant to defy social conventions that oppress entire generations of people.

Jesus, however, apparently did not set out to either do social action or to present a purely private and spiritual message of salvation. Evangelism and social concern were a seamless whole. At some points (such as denouncing the inequality of the divorce law) Jesus directly entered the legal and governmental realm. At most points, however, he moved at a depth-political level, reaching out to the individuals immediately around him in such a way that distorted social structures were exposed for what they were—harmful and relative human inventions, rather than the beneficial and absolute givens of God or nature.

To put it another way, he offered a new vision and a new identity. In his teaching and in the example of his life and death, Jesus provided the pattern for our own lives. By conforming our minds and bodies to his pattern, we will learn something of how the first shall be last and how the true self is found in service. We will see what is real; more than that, we will "know him who is real," the true God (1 John 5:20).

And if Jesus' pattern is correct, it will be as "we" and not as an isolated "I" that we come to know reality. In word and deed, Jesus called us to love God and neighbor (Mark 12:30–31). If we cannot love those we see with our eyes, it is impossible to love the unseen God (1 John 4:20). So this chapter, at its end, comes to one thing more that Jesus did: he created a new community.

4. The Church as Depth-Political Community

Since Jesus lived and died in the arid environs of Jerusalem, the world has changed many times over. Rome is no longer an empire, but an antique city. The Middle East remains troubled, but with new hatreds and more desperate divisions. People no longer believe the earth is the center of the universe. They have a name ("ego") and grand theory for the continuing human inclination to think the self is the center of the universe. There are ethical quandaries, such as nuclear deterrence and genetic engineering, that the rabbis of the first century could not have remotely imagined. Perhaps most significantly, in the centuries since Jesus, major parts of the world have evolved from to pre-Christian to Christian and now to post-Christian societies. What Christ can mean in a post-Christian world is no idle question; nor is it one only for esoteric academics. The farmer, the banker, and the shoe clerk wonder too: when so much has changed, what does Jesus mean for today?

The answer is not a proposition, but a people. What Jesus means for today is the church.

JESUS' NEW COMMUNITY

In the previous chapter we attempted to convey something of the originality and boldness of Jesus' challenge to the powers and the world. With his ministry he drew the outline of the kingdom: a rule of forgiveness and recognition of the parenthetical people. By his death and resurrection Jesus, the consummate depth politician, directly confronted and dethroned the powers that misguide individuals and societies. But still, as we also noted, evil and suffering clearly and abundantly remain. We live "between the times" of the cross and consummation of history. That leaves us with a key question: how is the victory of Christ over the powers effective in the present? How do Jesus and the kingdom make any difference at all?

In reply, the New Testament does not point to socio-political revolution (as might the religious Left) or to the nation America (as might the religious Right). It points to the church. The Letter to the Ephesians sees Jesus sitting at the right hand of the Father, ruling over all authority, dominion, and power (1:19–23). The means of this rule is the church, which continually proclaims Christ's victory. By its life the church persists in confronting the powers with the fact of their defeat. So, Ephesians has it, it is through the church that the "manifold wisdom of God" is "made known to the principalities and powers in the heavenly places" (3:10, RSV).

The New Testament's insistence that the church is the primary focus of God's activity in the world derives from the fact that Jesus came and inaugurated a kingdom—in his words, with his life, through his death. And he did not leave the reflection and manifestation of that kingdom to isolated individuals; he established a community. He called to himself twelve disciples, a sign of the New Israel (twelve tribes).[1] And from them grew the church, the ekklesia, which itself means "those called forth."[2]

The church is not a club where people with common hobbies meet. It is not a voluntary association, such as the American Medical Association, in which members guard and tend to their shared interests. Nor is it simply a helping organization, an Alcoholics Anonymous that people seek out after they determine they have an unmanageable problem. People choose to join AA or a civic club but, in that sense, no one really "joins" the church. The members of the church are called, gathered together by the God who showed himself in Jesus Christ.

In being gathered, they become participants in the work of Christ. The biblical language is stronger. The New Testament thinks of the church as Christ's body (1 Cor. 12:27); Christians are their Lord's limbs and organs (1 Cor. 6:15). It comes to no less than this: as Jesus' body the church holds within it "the fullness of him who himself receives the entire fullness of God" (Eph. 1:23).

THE CHURCH AND DEPTH-POLITICAL ETHICS

The church, then, is a real, visible, tangible manifestation of Jesus' presence in the world. Jesus identifies with the church. Caring for the naked, thirsty, and imprisoned among his brethren, he said, is tantamount to caring for him (Matt. 25:31–46). Similarly, he told Peter, "If you love me, feed my sheep" (John 21:15–17). Before sending his disciples on a mission he informed them, "Whoever rejects you rejects me" (Luke 10:16). And one from Tarsus, who had hounded and murdered Christians, was met by a bright light and a voice demanding, "Saul, Saul, why do you persecute me?" (Acts 9:4).

Because it is so clearly related to Christ, the church has astonishing claims made about it. Paul writes to the church at Corinth—the most disreputable in the entire New Testament, soiled with gluttony and incest—to tell it "everything belongs to you," including the wide world (1 Cor. 3:21–23). When the church at Colossae was perhaps seven years old, meeting in a few homes, Paul declared it had a part in the destiny of the universe (Col. 1:16–18).[3]

Reading with twentieth-century American eyes, we too easily convert these and other passages into individualistic Christianity. Yet the clear message of the New Testament is incontrovertible. When men and women are called to Christ, they are called into a community. The light of the world is a "city" (Matt. 5:14). Those who follow Christ are members of a "chosen race" and citizens of a "dedicated nation" (1 Pet. 2:9). The prayer they are taught to pray is addressed to "*Our* Father."

The ethic they are exhorted to live is basically not a private ethic, but a social ethic, a depth-political ethic meant to challenge the identities and visions of men and women compliant to the powers-controlled structures of the world. While passages such as Romans 12:9–21 can be lifted out of context and read individualistically, the exhortations to "practice hospitality" and "call down blessings on your persecutors" are addressed to a community. Likewise, the *personal* ethical guidance of Ephesians 4–6 is predicated on membership in the redeemed *community* outlined in the earlier chapters.[4]

Jesus' ethic is not intended for isolated individuals. It is an ethic for a new family, a circle of disciples, a people gathered by God. "Whether or not this ethic can be fulfilled is something that can only be determined by groups of people which consciously place themselves under the gospel of the reign of God and wish to be real communities of brothers and sisters—communities which form a living arena for faith."[5]

Amid the church and going out from it are those who live as Jesus lived, who plot their lives after the plot of the Jesus story and build their character after the characterization of the Jesus story. Ugly as it can be, run-down as it can get, the church is Jesus' body. "Jesus Christ exists as Community," Bonhoeffer said boldly.[6]

This, then, is how the question, "What does Jesus mean today?" is answerable. It cannot be answered by merely reciting a formula. It cannot be answered by simply pointing to a verse in the Bible. It cannot be answered by the counsel or example of any one person. But it can be answered by the comings and goings of a certain people in the world; by the worship, words, and deeds of a new society among the societies; by the depth politics of the church.

A DIACRITICAL COMMUNITY

We are suggesting that the church will have its intended and most powerful effect in the world not by attempting to direct government, but by moving and working at the deep social levels where identities and visions are formed. The church changes identities and visions by witnessing to and living by the story of Jesus, who saw the world as it is but refused to leave it that way. He did not challenge the world on its own terms, the terms of the sword, of domination and coercion. Instead, he took up a cross, a sign of service.

Significantly, the church is a community set free by the cross, and if it is to continue to manifest Jesus' presence in the world, it must live cruciformly—in the shape and after the pattern of the cross. By taking up the alternative identity and vision borne by its story and signified by the cross, the church becomes a community of people free from the powers and proclaims that freedom to all who see it. By living true to the sign of the cross, the church is itself a sign in the world, a sign that the powers of nations or revolutions are not ultimate and that death has its bounds.

The church, in other words, contradicts what the world takes to be reality. But the church's contradiction is no end in itself; the ultimate objective of its contradiction is to point to Christ. Just as the best doctor is not obsessed with sickness but keeps true health uppermost in her vision, the church contradicts the world "in a way which is full of promise."[7] It contradicts with the confidence that Christ is present to the world and offers it new life.

The church, then, is not simply a critical community, but a *diacritical community*. The critic calls attention to something wrong; *the diacritic goes one step beyond criticism and distinguishes an alternative.* Accordingly, the church intends not only to criticize and contradict the identities and visions of the world, but to present a distinctive, alternative identity and vision.

If this is so, one of the church's greatest dangers is to lose its alternative identity and vision, to blend itself with its surrounding society. Unfortunately, much of the church in contemporary North America does not understand itself as a diacritical community. The religious right especially tends to identify the essence of Christianity with American civil religion. And it does so at a time when civil religion has lost most of its influence and potency. At least the civil religion of the Middle Ages left religious potentates with the power to direct or effectively upbraid the civil authorities. Such power is reflected in the medieval legends that Pope Sylvester and the emperor Constantine exchanged documents ratifying one another's sovereignty, and that Archbishop Ambrose of Milan had disciplined the emperor Theodosius after a political massacre.

But Jerry Falwell cannot threaten Ronald Reagan with excommunication, nor can Pat Robertson effectively deny the legitimacy of Ted Kennedy's authority to legislate. Today there is no monolithic church that grants legitimacy to political authorities or disciplines them when they stray. Thus the civil religion so many cling to garnishes political authority with a patina of religious respectability, but it is ineffectual in significantly influencing the same authorities. When it accedes to civil religion the church has traded away its status as a light on the hill. The price of civil religion is quiet acquiescence to the will of the established powers.[8]

Civil religion has another cost. If the church fails to be a diacritical community, the world will not recognize itself. It will not understand that it is lost, drifting in chaos, operating in enmity with the God of all reality. The church's light is the elimination of darkness that reveals darkness for what it is. Without the provocation of the diacritical community the world is not only bereft of its true identity but has no opportunity to understand its true problem, its actual plight.

Rather than acquiescing to its outmoded role in the civil religious pageant, then, the church should strive to remain a diacritical community. Witnessing to the fullness of the kingdom, it can never be a satisfied community. It can accept no governmental or economical system as final and perfect. Its support of capitalism, socialism, or any other economic system is pragmatic and provisional. Its allegiance to America, Britain, or any other country is secondary and subordinated. Though it must responsibly support what it judges to be the most just system available, it must always be ready to stand against the abuses of any system and so to demonstrate that only the consummated kingdom is absolute.

As a diacritical community the church must also beware of a selective "prophetic ministry." Too often Christians who are prophetic about the nuclear arms race have nothing to say about pornography. And Christians who courageously oppose abortion on demand resist measures that would help women achieve equity in the marketplace. Of course, there is rarely a position on any particular issue that is the cut-and-dried Christian position. Thus the diacritical community must always be suspicious of the possibility that a political or economic agenda—rather than the story of Jesus—is determining its agenda. As sociologist Peter Berger suggests, "Do not call yourself a prophet if your hometown agrees with you."[9]

What shape, then, is taken by a diacritical community, one based on the story of Jesus? What does it mean to say that a community lives and dies cruciformly? It means this community takes as its way of life and death the example and empowerment of Christ. The church bears and witnesses to the sign of the cross by *being* the sign of the cross. And there are four important ways it is this sign to the world: by being a community of giftedness, by being an eschatological community, by being a community of forgiven-ness, and by being a community of presence.

A COMMUNITY OF GIFTEDNESS

Before and after all else, the church is a community of giftedness. It is no collection of extraordinary men and women; it is only a people awakened to the fact that to know the world is to know a gift. The church confesses that the world is not self-created. The Lord "hath made us, and not we ourselves" (Ps. 100:3, KJV). So the church has in itself nothing to boast about. It is simply a community trying to live in the realization that the entire creation depends on God's self-giving.

The church comes to this realization through Christ: God "did not spare his own Son, but gave him up for us all; and with this gift how can he fail to lavish upon us all he has to give?" (Rom. 8:32). The cross, furthermore, is a sign of Christ's generosity: for the sake of humanity "he who was rich beyond all means became poor, and through his poverty we have been made rich" (2 Cor. 8:9). Through the cross the church learns that life is a gift and that to live is to give. By being a community of giftedness, it is truly diacritical.

First, it can only see creation as a gift to be enjoyed and cultivated, rather than a possession to be exploited. The church does not share the technological virtues of utility and efficiency. It cannot see the forest, like technology does, only as so many rolls of paper or stacks of lumber. It understands creation to have a life of its own right and that by being what they were made to be, flora and fauna themselves praise God and his generosity (see Ps. 148–150).

Second, the community of giftedness is composed of persons who have learned they do not own themselves. Their lives are not self-controlled and self-managed, but given up to their Giver. The church is a community of people happy to confess, "We do not belong to ourselves: we were bought at a price" (1 Cor. 6:10–20). Therefore, Christians, in diacritical witness, release their tightened, positive grip on self and open that self to the surprises of God that come in the guise of the stranger and the enemy. A community of giftedness is a community of hospitality.

And third, persons in the community of giftedness recognize they have been given one another. The riches of Christ cannot be realized in any single individual. The depth and variety of Christ's gifts are appreciated only in his body, in depending on and helping one another. To enjoy a friend in Christ is to enjoy Christ, to suffer with a friend in Christ is to suffer with Christ, to learn more about a friend in Christ is to learn more about Christ.

Diacritically, then, the church is not a loose collection of highly independent individuals. The Spirit was given to build up the body of Christ. Once again the church is done a disservice if Scripture is read individualistically. The gifts of the Holy Spirit are given to integrate and strengthen the body. As Paul writes to the Corinthians, even the greatest of these gifts (love) amounts to nothing if the body is not built up (1 Cor. 14:17). The individual edifies or builds up himself only as he edifies the community. This might be called Paul's criterion of solidarity: the goodness and appropriateness of an ability or gift is gauged by whether or not it builds up the body.

In addition to being edified by gifts, the community is built up by the fruits, or character, given to it by the Holy Spirit. Peace, patience, self-control, and the other virtues (Gal. 5:22–23) are the results of the individual living ethically within and for the community. This she does after the example of Christ: "Each of us must consider his neighbor and think what is good and will build up the common life. For Christ too did not consider himself" (Rom. 15:2–3).[10]

Living under the sign of the cross, the community of giftedness is a healed and restored body and, living under the sign of the cross, the church becomes a sign that one day the entire world will be healed and restored. As Karl Barth astutely notes, the New Testament never uses the term "body" of humanity as a whole, but only of the Christian community. In that community there is now wholeness, wholeness in the "dispensing and eating of the bread which is broken in common."[11] Under the sign of the cross, the church recognizes that wholeness for creation, self, and others lies solely in Christ. Consequently, what it owes to the world is to be the church, to be whole in Christ today in anticipation of the world's wholeness in Christ tomorrow.

AN ESCHATOLOGICAL COMMUNITY

To say that the church is presently whole in anticipation of the world's future wholeness is one way of saying the church is an eschatological community. This does not mean the church has a detailed calendar of the world's end. More profoundly, it means that the story of Jesus reveals the goal and purpose of history. Christ is the alpha and the omega, the beginning and the end (Rev. 21:6), and his story reveals that the world is in the hands of a loving God and is moving toward a new heaven and a new earth. The church anticipates the day when Christ's victory over the powers will be crowned, when nature will no longer be bloodied in disharmony and nations will no longer war.

But the church's eschatological knowledge is not an esoteric, gnostic secret that grants it pride and power. The church's aim is not to build a political power base and direct the course of nations. Rather, the church intends to be a community where the peace of God's kingdom begins. In this sense the church is the beginning of the future of the world.

Beginnings are essential. There is no mature woman without the baby girl coming first. The building exists only if the first brick was laid. But beginnings are not to be confused with their endings or final goals: the woman is more complex than the baby girl, the building more impressive than its first brick. So, too, may the church be compared to the restored world. The church is precious and necessary, yet the restored earth will be more beautiful and admirable. The church begins to stagnate the second it thinks it has reached perfection or maturity, even in the single detail. Just as we are distressed if the baby girl remains an infant and disappointed if the building never grows beyond a few bricks, we should not act as if the church is the complete arrival of the new creation.

As an eschatological community, the church always has its eyes on the end. It is unique among earthly communities in that it has its roots in the future and its branches in the present.[12] It lives now in anticipation of the kingdom's consummation. It lives now in the strength and awareness of the kingdom that will one day be complete. This means the community can live confidently and creatively.

It lives *confidently* because its roots, sure and deep, are in the future, the future in which God's rule will be recognized by all. The book of Revelation is an exhortation to the beleaguered church to remember that victory belongs to the Lamb (e.g., Rev. 7:10). The church can live in faith that the future is in God's control. In such faith the church is a diacritical community, living "out of control" and not attempting—in contrast to the rest of the world—to manage history.

The eschatological community lives *creatively* for the same reason that it lives confidently: it lives by faith. Faith does not concern things seen, substances that can be possessed and used like chunks of coal or matters that lie within human determination (Heb. 11:1–3). Faith is trust; it is a gift of One who has shown himself to be trustworthy in the story of Israel and Christ. The church in no way controls or comprehends God.

This means that God may not only surprise the world—he may surprise the church. The eschatological community sees God in Christ, but it sees him partially, as in the reflections in a dusky mirror (1 Cor. 13:12). Oddly, the disciples who were most intimate with Jesus did not immediately recognize him when he appeared to them following his resurrection. Christ is a stranger to Cleopas and his companion on the road to Emmaus. Not realizing who they are talking to, they express their despair and disappointment about the crucified man—"We had hoped that he was the one to redeem Israel" (Luke 24:21, RSV)—and so demonstrate that they did not fully understand redemption or the crucified one. So, too, the original disciples are back at their fishing boats, where they first met Jesus, when the resurrected Lord appears to them. It is as if they must go back to the beginning and learn afresh to know and understand him.[13]

That the community never knows Christ completely or finally means that it must live creatively. It can face the challenges that new times bring: the ethical dilemmas of advanced sciences such as genetic engineering, the ministerial problems of cities larger and more concentrated than ever before, the constant tumbles and ascents of every human culture. Exactly because it is an eschatological community, the church must be willing to move from the "destructively familiar to the creatively strange."[14] Of course the church treasures its tradition, its very life-source, but it cannot rightly use that living tradition as an excuse for an uncritical attempt at returning to the past or for endorsing any status quo merely for the sake of comfort and security. To meet Jesus is to encounter one who "evades our surface desires and surface needs, and will not subserve the requirements of our private dramas."[15]

The church is diacritical by not clinging to old and routine ways, using the channels of power to retain power and the assurance of continued security in a precarious world. Instead, it countenances the strangeness and newness of tomorrow, because it trusts tomorrow's Lord. An eschatological community can risk failure. To meet Jesus means to learn that we have not arrived but only begun, that we will repeatedly (though we hope creatively) fail and so stand in continual need of forgiveness.

THE COMMUNITY OF FORGIVEN-NESS

The world is a place of cyclical violence. An individual is hurt physically or emotionally, and so she hurts another in return. Sometimes she responds directly to the one who hurt her. At other times, especially when the one who hurt her is more powerful, she strikes out at those who are less powerful. What is true of individuals is no less true of nations. The defeated Germany of World War I rose up as the defeating Germany of World War II. In a significant sense violence never "settles" anything—it only shifts, for a time, the burden of who will inflict pain and who will suffer. The sufferer may change, but violence is guaranteed to go on and on.

That is, it is guaranteed to go on unless someone chooses to forgive. Forgiveness frees both those who forgive and those forgiven. Those who forgive refuse to perpetuate the cycle of violence and are liberated to turn from destructive living to constructive living. The ones forgiven no longer have to worry about spiteful retaliation and can drop their guard; they, too, can turn their energies from the power to destroy to the power to build up.

What a searing self-rebuke it is, then, when the church fights and hates among itself. Christians of the political Left and Right betray their primary allegiance to political ideologies when they fail to recognize one another in Christ. It is dangerous when a Christian of the political Left suggests that one cannot be a "true Christian" and support the Strategic Defense Initiative, or when a Christian of the political Right wonders how a "true Christian" could have voted for the Panama Canal Treaty. However history may judge the rightness or wrongness of a particular political stand, the church in the present is called to be a zone of neutrality.

Just as Jesus called radical zealots and establishment tax collectors into his circle, the church of today should be a place where Christians of all political persuasions gather at the feet of their common Lord. Surely this will not fail to have an incidental political effect, for how often do hostile opponents really listen to one another?

Of course, inside or outside the community, it takes tremendous courage to be those who forgive, for those who forgive are the first to lay down their physical swords or psychological shields. The church is the community that forgives because it is first the community of forgiven-ness.[16] "Be forbearing with one another, and forgiving, where any of you has cause for complaint: you must forgive as the Lord forgave you" (Col. 3:13). The people of the church have the courage to forgive because they have already been forgiven. Christians can drop their guard because he who is most powerful, the creator and judge of all, has chosen to forgive. As scholar Paul Hanson writes, "True human community is created only where the community between God and humans is restored."[17] Reconciliation with our fellow human beings is based on and grows out of reconciliation with God. Thus the church can take no pride in itself when it forgives. It can forgive only because it is the community of giftedness and is gifted with forgiveness. Christians are apprentices in forgiveness, learning to forgive just as Christ forgave them. The church is a diacritical community by forgiving rather than perpetuating violence.

Besides enabling it to interrupt the cycle of violence, the church's forgiven-ness lends to it a special sense of realism about sin and tragedy in the world. The church knows that forgiveness was and is costly in a violent world: Christ on the cross is the cost of forgiveness written on a human face and body. Quite apart from any physical danger, living under the sign of the cross is costly to our own pride, for it means admitting hostility, selfishness, and evil within ourselves. We once were enemies of God and often still are, in spite of our best intentions. Thus, every time the church asks for forgiveness it acknowledges the depth and tenacity of evil and admits the persistence of that evil in its presence.

Knowing the cost of divine forgiveness, the community takes forgiveness with deadly seriousness. It can never forget that it will be the first to be judged (1 Pet. 4:17). It realizes that if it does not take seriously the plea, "Lord, have mercy," the world never will. This is one more reason for the church's unending humility, for its once-and-for-all renunciation of triumphalism. The church is truly diacritical by admitting its own tragic sinfulness. How much easier it is for nations, tribes, families, and individuals to point to others as the source of evil. By acknowledging its own sin, the diacritical community not only interrupts the spiral of violence, but the spiral of blame that leads to violence.

Finally, the community's forgiven-ness is what grants it true, diacritical hope. We live at a time when some Christians tend toward cynicism and despair. They see only the grim edifice of materialism, the towering stockpile of nuclear weapons, and the gathering tidal wave of national debt. They are profoundly skeptical that the world will be changed in any significant way. They especially doubt that they and a handful of other Christians can make any public difference and so are liable to a privatistic Christianity that seeks to gain something for self, but is apathetic about others and resigned about the fate of the earth.

Other Christians indulge in shallow optimism. For them, secular humanism and communism are the source of all ills. They believe that once Christians are in control (presumably bolstering the military budget and restoring prayer to schools), all will be well. America need only return to its supposed heritage and a rainbow will arc around the world.

True hope, however, is born of forgiven-ness and admits the enduring reality of evil and sin within others *and ourselves*. Yet it also trusts that the God of renewing grace will offer his grace again and again. The community of forgiven-ness can celebrate truly and mourn truly. In a gifted but suffering world it possesses a prismatic joy that denies neither gift nor deprivation, a joy that gains depth and color only when refracted through tears. Forgiven, the community takes courage to look on the world *and itself* as they really are. Its hope is diacritical, opting neither for cynicism or shallow optimism. It recognizes the world and the community as they really are but struggles to see them changed in the grace of God. So it is that the community of forgiven-ness at once has the greatest commitment to reality—to seeing what actually exists—and yet strikes up the greatest rebellion against reality on behalf of what can be.[18]

THE COMMUNITY OF PRESENCE

God evidenced his presence to the world in his historical actions on behalf of Israel and in the person and work of Christ. As the Old Testament scholar Christopher J. H. Wright affirms, God is not concerned with righteousness and justice as abstract ideas. In the Bible, these are "highly personal and relational terms. Theologically, they characterize God in action in relationship with men—men at large, and especially his people. Socially, they are required of people in their relationship with one another."[19]

The incarnation proves that the grace and love of God are not abstract, but personal. God is not simply an amorphous and passionless spiritual existence, a "divine principle" or "unmoved mover." He wills to be present to humanity in all its particularity. "Jesus, it must be remembered, restricted nine-tenths of his ministry to twelve Jews because it was the only way to redeem all Americans. He couldn't be bothered . . . with the foreign Canaanites because his work was to save the whole world."[20]

Likewise, the community of presence cannot simply refer to God as an idea or elaborate doctrine. It makes God real by telling the world the story of God's intervention on its behalf and by embodying God's love and justice in the world. Of course, every society holds up love and justice as ideals, and each has its own definitions and standards of love and justice. The church is unique in that it learns what love and justice are from the story of Israel and Jesus.

At the very least, as we have already indicated, this means that it rejects love as a mere principle. It insists on the particularity of love. It doubts that a man loves women if he fails to love his wife, or that a woman truly cares for children if she neglects her daughter. The community of presence is not a sprawling, impersonal bureaucracy. It recognizes the inevitability of bureaucracy in mass society but never confuses bureaucratic efficiency for true Christian love.

In her novel *Final Payments*, Mary Gordon keenly contrasts bureaucratic efficiency with love that dares to be genuinely present. Her heroine is a fledgling social worker assigned to visit the homes of citizens who were paid to house and care for elderly people. When the novice suggests social workers should enter sensitively into the homes and lives of others, she is informed, "You're there to get information, not to make friends." She muses that the bureaucrats might pay attention to the details of care that make the elderly happy, only to hear such attention reduced to "efficiency analysis." Later, upon visiting several homes, she observes that some of the cleanest, most "efficient" places are operated by families that have no human warmth for the elderly in their houses. These families keep the elderly because they need the money.

But one place the young social worker visits is different. It is an unkempt home populated by several older people. While the social worker distributes forms to the elderly ones, the owner of the home retreats to the kitchen and weeps because one in her charge is dying of cancer. "It's Alice," she says, "I can't stand it . . . , knowing she's not going to be around." This is the one home the social worker visited to which she wished she could return. But, she realizes, "You [don't] walk into people's lives carrying a briefcase, carrying forms, and then go back again as if you were just another person."[21]

The bureaucrat cannot be present, attending as one person attends another. The community of presence is a community of people learning the tender art of being present to the people of the world, but especially to one another. They concentrate on being present to their companions in the community not because they regard the people of the world as less worthy, but because they know that presence is learned only in particularity and that they can be present to the world only to the degree they have learned to be present to one another.

Presence within the community does not replace governmental politics, since structural injustices within the society at large must be righted. Yet the significance of a community of people who are present to one another should not be underestimated. Presence within the community is depth politics, a politics that forms a vital community capable of changing the world. The church, as a diacritical community, gathers and lives in the name of and explicitly after the example of Christ, who alone has stripped the powers of their illusive supremacy. To live as a community of true presence is to be a sign to the world that a people can care for one another and live without ultimate allegiance to the powers and their care.

Far from being a "withdrawal" from the world and politics, this is the most direct and profoundly engaging political action any community can undertake. It is the demonstration of the possibility of a new vision and a new identity, a surprising and creative cruciform vision and identity. But however profound a witness the presence of the church may be, it can be summed up quite concisely: "In a word, as God's dear children, try to be like him, and live in love as Christ loved you, and gave himself up on your behalf" (Eph. 5:1–2).

THE PROMISE OF THE DIACRITICAL COMMUNITY

The church, first and foremost, is a diacritical community. It presents the world with the promise of contradiction in its giftedness, its eschatological identity, its forgiven-ness, and its presence. Through the community Christians hand down the story of Israel and Jesus, teaching this story "not only with our lips, but in our lives."[22] In community Christians encourage and hold one another accountable before their Lord. They complement one another's gifts, providing a fuller and more compelling reflection of Christ in the world.

As in the period of its inception, the church now exists in a world drained of meaning, fragmented to the desperate point that many despair of its reintegration. As in that ancient period, with the Roman Empire crumbling, many retreat to the consolations of private peace, attainment, and comfort. The strength of the early church was that it refused private salvation and learned how to live as the community of giftedness. As the eminent historian Peter Brown writes, "While the oriental cults provided special means to salvation in the next world, they took the position of their devotees in this world for granted." The church, while certainly expecting salvation in the next world, "offered a way of living in this world." The appeal of Christianity, Brown believes, "lay in its radical sense of community."[23]

It was a sense of community, of identity and vision granted by the story of Christ, that once changed the world. Who is to say it cannot do so again?

5. Worship and Depth Politics

If, as we have argued, the church's greatest service is to regain and live from its distinctive identity and vision, we are presented with the obvious question: How? What resources has the church that will renew its identity and vision, enabling it to be a significant and potent depth-political body?

The answer lies in the church's one unique and utterly distinctive action—its worship. In the words of Vatican II, "The liturgy is the summit toward which the activity of the church is directed; it is also the fount from which all her power flows."[1] Not all denominations call what they do on Sunday morning "liturgy," but every denomination has a form and order of worship. In that sense, all are "liturgical." Furthermore, all derive their identities and visions from the story of Israel and Christ, a story proclaimed in preaching and enacted in the sacraments of baptism and the Eucharist.

Contemporary liturgical scholarship, both Catholic and Protestant, has rediscovered the radical nature of worship, worship as it was understood by the primitive Christian community. Far from being a lecture hall exercise, an aesthetic experience for artistic types, or a mystical experience for romantics, worship is the fullest, most concentrated enactment of what the church is and will be. As Aidan Kavanagh comments, it is nothing less than the "the church's faith in motion."[2]

Such is the gist of this chapter: worship, or liturgy, is the church's distinctive and indispensable activity. It is the celebration of Christ's work shaping the character of a people who journey toward the new heaven and the new earth. Reconstituting identity and granting vision, worship is the fount from which all the church's depth-political power flows.

THE DANGERS OF WORSHIP

Worship is dangerous. It is not a retreat from reality, but a direct engagement with ultimate reality: God. Genuine worship is a response to God and what he has done; in it we make ourselves vulnerable to the story of Israel and Jesus. Sham worship attempts to manipulate and transform God, but true worship praises God *as he is* and calls Christians to risk the transformation of themselves and the world. "Does anyone have the foggiest idea of what sort of power we so blithely invoke?" Annie Dillard asks. "The churches are children playing on the floor with their chemistry sets, mixing up a batch of TNT to kill a Sunday morning. It is madness to wear ladies' straw hats and velvet hats to church; we should be all wearing crash helmets. Ushers should issue life preservers and signal flares; they should lash us to our pews."[3]

Let us make it perfectly clear that worship is not instrumental—it is not undertaken for the purpose of changing ourselves, individually or socially. Worship cannot be reduced to psychological therapy or political consciousness-raising. It is first and finally the service of God and needs no other justification. The transformation of worshipers is not its central aim. In fact, we are not apt to be changed by worship if we come to it primarily to be changed, for then we will be back to concentrating on ourselves. However noble our purposes, we will once again find ourselves attempting to manipulate God. The purposes (political, psychological, or otherwise) we bring to the liturgy define "reality." God becomes a benevolent and agreeable divine psychotherapist or Democrat or Communist. The story of Freud and Rogers, Jefferson and Franklin, or Marx and Lenin—whichever one we have found most agreeable and have made most predictable—is made the backbone and lifeblood of what we call worship. And the world is not changed. It only sees itself reflected in a pious mirror.

Liturgy (the work of the church for the world) is harder. It is practice at conformity to a difficult, revealed reality. Over and over again, it repeats, remembers, and reenacts the strange and surprising story of Israel and Jesus. It is not a mirror, but truly original art. And like an art, it demands that its practitioners bend themselves to its rules and submit themselves to its forms. The church's central aim in worship is to gratefully acknowledge reality. The transformation of the church is a by-product of the liturgy. It occurs only when the church is determined foremost simply to worship God.

But transformation is a significant by-product. It is all the more

significant because it is a by-product with both individual and social effects. What God has done in the story of Israel and Jesus
affected both individuals and societies. Therefore, if we respond
to the story in its fullness, depth politics will occur: the transformation of individuals and societies is inevitable. In the following
pages, then, we want to focus on this inevitable transformation.
There are, of course, three main actions in worship. Baptism and
the Eucharist (the Lord's Supper) are two. We begin with the
third, preaching, since it is the liturgical action most widely expected to form a new and different people.

PREACHING

At its most elemental, preaching does what the liturgy does. It
celebrates the story of Christ, who has introduced the kingdom
and defeated the principalities and powers. These powers have
distorted the vision and identity of humanity: the liturgy (and
preaching within it) means to establish the kingdom, the source of
true identity and vision.

This means that social and political issues do not lie at the heart
of preaching. The good news of the kingdom inaugurated and
the powers defeated is the heart of preaching.

Perhaps the most prominent threat to contemporary preaching
is the marketing model. The preacher who adopts the marketing
model imagines himself to be a salesman and the gospel to be a
product. (Thus Robert Schuller worries that if people do not respond to the gospel we may be "forced to say . . . that we have a
poor product.")[4] Most damagingly, the marketing model turns
the worshiping congregation into a "market" that must be ca-
tered to; from there it is only a short step to tailoring the gospel to
a congregation's perceived wants and politics. The right-wing
preacher will present a thoroughly capitalist and anticommunist
Christ; the left-wing preacher will offer up a socialist and anti-
capitalist Christ.

Rather than being adapted to fit a marketing model or political
agenda—our simple and finally unchallenged preconceptions—
preaching should proclaim a gospel that is never quite manage-
able, never adaptable to the "best laid plans of mice and men."

In one of his more stimulating essays, Walker Percy imagines an island castaway.[5] The castaway is amnesiac. He cannot remember the shipwreck or who he is, but the island is pleasant and populated and the castaway is resourceful. He finds a job, meets and marries a woman, and enjoys movies and concerts.

He also takes to walking the beach early each morning, and there he routinely comes across bottles washed ashore. In the bottle are slips of paper bearing a variety of messages such as:

Lead melts at 330 degrees.
Chicago, a city, is on Lake Michigan.
The market for eggs in Bora Bora [a neighboring island] is very good.
There is fresh water in the next cave.
A war party is approaching from Bora Bora.

Being curious and intelligent, the castaway categorizes the messages. Some, he notices, are messages of observation, *Lead melts at 330 degrees*, for example, or *Chicago, a city, is on Lake Michigan*. They are not especially radical or important. The islands, using their own sciences of chemistry and geography, can arrive at the same knowledge.

But other messages are immediately important, such as *There is fresh water in the next cave, The market for eggs in Bora Bora is very good*, or *A war party is approaching from Bora Bora*. As Percy notes, "These sentences are highly significant to the islander, because he is thirsty, because he is in the egg business, or because his island society is threatened." These messages Percy calls "news."

"The hearer of news," Percy writes, "is a man who finds himself in a predicament. News is precisely that communication which has bearing on his predicament and is therefore good or bad news." News is "delivered to be heeded and acted upon." A man dying of thirst will not consider the information that there are diamonds on the next dune real news, but he will consider directions to a nearby oasis crucial news and will certainly act on it.

For Percy, knowledge is one thing and news is another. He means the story of the castaway to be analogous to the situation of humanity. We are all castaways, capable of gathering knowledge, creating art and science, but not knowing by our most magnificent arts and sciences where we have come from or who we ultimately are. In this predicament, the gospel is news—very good news.

Preaching means telling the story of the gospel in such a way that it is news—or rather that it *remains* news. It is, after all, news of the most crucial kind. It ceases to be news only when the preacher distorts it and tames the gospel to make it more palatable to his hearers.

Such preaching, whether of the religious Right or Left, is ultimately a safe and unthreatening moralism. The problem with moralism is that it focuses not on what God has done, does, and will do, but on what we can do. Whereas moralism seeks to "domesticate the faith and tame the Christian life into socially approved conduct," the preaching of the undistorted gospel proclaims God is greater than any of our human constructs.[6] Moralistic preaching may be temporarily and mildly discomforting, but it finally calls people to duties they are capable of fulfilling entirely on their own. The preacher who tells the story of Israel and Jesus radically displaces all human effort and puts God at the center. She causes people to focus their attention on and adore Christ, knowing, as Augustine said, "We become what we adore."

Preaching, then, is a matter of forming identity and vision. The gospel is light, but a blinded man must gain sight before he can see the light. The constant temptation of the preacher will be to succumb to the marketing model and offer the blind a darkness they call light. Harder and truer preaching gives vision. Nonmoralistic preaching makes the community conscious of grace (and consequently of sin as well). By telling the story of the gospel, it shapes a people who see by the light of the gospel and act in it. They gain compassion because they can see those in need. They gain peace and can discern violence where others miss it. Sacrifice on behalf of others, rather than a degradation of self, comes to be seen as the true fulfillment of self.

We might turn from the visual metaphor and state it another way: preaching forms a community capable of hearing God's word and doing it. Or, again, we might turn from the metaphors of sight and sound to a third expression: preaching develops a taste for the duties and character of the Christian life. But these "duties" are created and empowered by the love of God. Thus Christians can rightly say "another name for duty is love." Preaching aims to "make us love God, or rather, help us to believe in his love for us."[7]

To help us believe in God's love for us, preaching must be relevant to our predicament. The preacher makes the word of God immediate and alive. He preaches to a particular congregation: in Omaha he is conscious of the farm crisis, in Amarillo he takes into account the moral dilemma of working for a weapons contractor. Such preaching is prophetic, not dulling the sharp edge of the gospel but allowing it to cut into the lives of the people. Preaching certainly can and often should be consolatory, yet always within the grammar and terms of the story of Israel and Jesus—it lifts the sufferers to a new way of seeing and understanding their pain.

To preach this way demands a credible newsbearer. It means that preaching is a communal endeavor, in that the preacher must be present and responsible to his people. He, too, must hear the demands and exult in the joys of the gospel. He must allow it to be news for him and not merely passionless knowledge (like the datum that lead melts at 330 degrees). Amid genuine suffering, the preacher will not be allowed to reduce the gospel to an abstract, cold formula. In this sense, visits to jails and hospitals may do more to foster good preaching than the finest homiletics course.

Preaching, like the liturgy in general, cannot be separated from life and mission. The preacher will be a credible newsbearer when the congregation knows she has the courage to challenge her own predilections in her sermons and when she struggles, in its presence, to admit the challenging love and ultimacy of God in all of existence. In William Willimon's words, "The sermon is a humble, prayerful effort by the preacher to articulate the truth and then to allow the naked truth to stand equally against congregation and preacher."[8]

Preaching, in short, is the proclamation of reality. Retelling the Christian story of the kingdom's coming and the powers' defeat, it challenges its hearers to embrace a new identity and new vision. It calls the people of God to its provocative status as a diacritical community, reminding and emboldening it to live out its new vision and identity at home, in the workplace, and in the public square.

BAPTISM

Supposedly reporters once approached Martha Graham, the founder of modern dance, and asked her, "Miss Graham, what does your dance mean?" She is said to have replied, "Darlings, if I could tell you I would not have danced it."[9]

The situation is similar when we attempt to bring words to the sacraments of baptism and the Eucharist. We can only use words to poke at and toy with these mysteries; ultimately they surpass description and have to be "danced." Yet we can at least hint at the richness of the sacraments and suggest how they help Christians to live their entire life after the pattern of the Christ story. How does baptism shape and inform the new identity and vision of the diacritical community?

Like preaching, baptism does what the entire liturgy does. It reenacts the death and resurrection of Christ, making present and real all the promise of the new world gained in that death and resurrection. With bodily gestures, use of material elements, and words, baptism is the initiation of the entire person into the story of Israel and Jesus. It is an enactment or drama of the entire history, from creation to resurrection.

The water of baptism is a primal symbol of germination. "Water was the first to produce that which had life," wrote the church father Tertullian. Taking and blessing water, the sacrament draws creation into its drama. No less does the use of water symbolize the Fall and chaos, for water is also an agent of disintegration. Early Christians considered submersion in the baptismal water akin to submersion in the destructive waters of the Noahic flood.[10]

Jewish baptism, which Christian baptism assumes, also connected baptism with the Exodus and the hope for a second, ultimate exodus. Thus Isaiah imagined a time when God would "clear a highway through the desert," just as he once did for his people Israel, and reveal his glory across the earth (Isa. 40:3, 5).

Of course our baptism is also a sign of Jesus' own baptism: first his water baptism and then his baptism by death. In being baptized by water—over John's protest—Jesus identified with those he came to save. At the least Jesus' water baptism means that he accepted the story of Israel for himself; he took Israel's crossing of the Jordan as his own crossing, implying that God was at work in the history of this people and that Jesus' own work, if it was to be authentic, had to flow from Israel's history. Later Jesus spoke of his impending death as a baptism (Mark 10:32–45), a death he had to die to defeat death and sin. When we are baptized we are baptized into Christ's death (Rom. 6:3), but also (and thankfully) into his resurrection (Rom. 6:5). To be baptized is to lay Christ's entire life story over the grid of our life story: we are co-buried (Rom. 6:4), co-grown (6:4–5), co-crucified (6:6), and we co-live with Christ (6:8).[11]

We can imagine how long it would take simply to read the biblical story from creation to consummation. Yet baptism, a remarkably compact ceremony, leaves none of the story out. By including but not relying on words alone, the sacrament has the advantage of involving the entire person: mind, body, and heart. Baptism is participation—intelligent, full-bodied, wholehearted participation. The Jew of Jesus' time required converted Gentiles to be baptized because one had to participate in the Jewish story to be a Jew.[12] This participation was a serious matter, since once you left Egypt there was no turning back, however preferable the old slavery (and fleshpots) had come to seem. To take a new story is to take a new life.

The original Christians understood baptism with an equal degree of sobriety, as a matter of life and death, an awesome initiation that thrust them straightaway into the "storm center of the universe."[13] The sacrament is no less profound today. We are only baptized once, but the sacrament takes a lifetime to finish. It signifies that Christians are made, not born, so that each day will require of us the extension and revivification of our baptism. The sacrament of baptism is the Christian introduction to the lifelong drama of repentance and conversion. Giving us a new story and a new identity, it has unending ramifications for our personal, social, and political lives.

The first and most important implication of baptism is the formation of a diacritical community, the church. Baptism initiates the individual into a community that takes its identity from the death and resurrection of Christ. With a new identity, the Christian is reoriented to the world. To bless and submit to the water of baptism is to admit that the physical creation is a good gift of God. It is intended to mediate his love and good will to humanity. Baptism also makes the church a royal nation and all Christians priests (1 Pet. 2:9; Rev. 1:6; 5:10). The stars, sun and moon, fire, water, and all else give God praise by being what they are (see Ps.

148) and, like humanity, await the consummation of the kingdom that will end all disharmony (Rom. 8:22–23). As priests we are called to the privilege of articulating the creation's inarticulate praise of God. Baptism calls us to a way of life respectful of creation and responsible to humanity's priestly stewardship of it. Christians who are true to their baptism will be seriously concerned with maintaining a balanced and bountiful ecology.

Baptism not only reorients the individual toward nature, but toward society. "To be incorporated into Christ's death and resurrection means to be grafted into the Body of Christ, to be initiated into a faith which is essentially a way of living together."[14] By drawing us into a community and "a way of living together," baptism refutes unchecked individualism. It teaches us first to consider the needs of others and to work for the upbuilding of the body as a whole. It demonstrates that there is no self-made man or woman, at least not in the most radical sense of receiving God's grace.

Consequently, baptism has often been called the sacrament of equality. Discrimination on the basis of sex, class, race—baptism obliterates it all. "Baptized into union with him, you have all put on Christ as a garment. There is no such thing as Jew and Greek, slave and freeman, male and female, for you are all one person in Christ Jesus," Paul writes (Gal. 3:27–28). Baptism is the basis of social justice, "For indeed we were all brought into one body by baptism, in one Spirit, whether we are Jews or Greeks, whether slaves or free men, and that one Holy Spirit was poured out for all of us to drink" (1 Cor. 12:13).

In this fashion baptism not only constitutes and creates a community in a fragmented world but shapes a community of equals in an unjust world. Writing the community into the story of Jesus, it expects the community to adopt the character of Jesus. As Paul indicates in Galatians 3:27, baptism is the act of putting on Christ as a garment. In Colossians 3:12–13, he uses the same baptismal language: "Then put on the garments that suit God's chosen people, his own, his beloved: compassion, kindness, humility, gentleness, patience. Be forebearing with one another, and forgiving where any of you has cause for complaint: you must forgive as the Lord forgave you. . . . Whatever you are doing, whether you speak or act, do everything in the name of the Lord Jesus, giving thanks to God the Father through him." Such is life as liturgy after the liturgy, with Christ as the pattern setter for individual and social ethics.

Baptism is especially significant because life after this act of liturgy is life after death. Entrance into Christ's death and resurrection is the most important aspect of baptism in the New Testament.[15] It is this aspect of baptism that vividly reminds us faith is a risk. Baptism might also be called the sacrament of letting go, since after it, "We must now live as dead people who have given up hope in ourselves and the old certainties, people who have let go."[16] The community of the baptized is a community that must live by God's surprises: it has dared to leave Egypt, to pick up the cross. This community has braved death and found new life.

Storyteller Garrison Keillor writes about one Sveeggen, a farm boy of twelve, who was left alone one Saturday evening while the rest of the family went to town. As Sveeggen was in the barn finishing the chores, a severe blizzard engulfed the farm. Looking out the barn door, he "was sure he saw a ghostly mass of house and black roof ahead and so he plunged into the blizzard and was blinded by white light and everything disappeared." Frantically taking steps in every direction and finding only more air, empty except for the swirling snow, the boy knew he was lost and was going to die.

Then the house caught fire. Seeing the orange glow, he walked toward it and warmed himself by the blaze. Regaining his bearings, he then "ran straight into the blizzard and ran smack into the side of the barn, where he spent the night, lying next to the cow, Tina, holding his broken nose." Living into old age, Sveeggen never forgot this direct and terrifying confrontation with death. Like Christians undergoing baptism, he responded gratefully—"How kind is God the Father, we were all lost in sin"—changed and free forever after.

Having lost his life he entered the new one with a sweet disposition. He planted trees, raised cattle, married, had seven children, and seldom spoke a harsh word. His nose was never set. He pitched ten tons of hay the day he was married; in their wedding picture, he sits, smiling, his eyes bright beside his ruined beak, a man who took a hard wallop and now everything was easy for him.[17]

The baptized ones, like the young man who perished in the snow yet lived to rear seven children, have died to their old identities and lived to gain a new identity. No longer do they depend on the powers and the principalities for an identity. They cannot be finally defined by nationality, race, political affiliation, level of consumerism, class, intelligence quotient, or any other institution and practice susceptible to the leverage of the powers. If the final threat of any power is death, what sway has a power over people who have already confronted death in the death of Christ, and begun to live by the resurrection of Christ? The church, therefore, is a people with a new identity and an astonishing freedom. It was the new identity and freedom of baptism that gave the black church the strength and motivation to struggle for justice. It was the new identity and freedom of baptism that gave Karl Barth and the other cosigners of the Barmen Declaration strength and motivation to stand against the Nazi war machine.

Though they do not all have broken noses like Sveeggen, all Christians are marked. At baptism they are sealed in a diacritical community (Eph. 1:13), set apart and freed to live out its purposes.

EUCHARIST

Like preaching and baptism, the Eucharist does what the liturgy does. Taking up elements of the Jewish Passover, it reenacts the story of Christ's cross and resurrection, anticipating the messianic age when all pain and sorrow is ended.

Baptism draws us into the story of Israel and Christ. Though we grow into it daily and affirm it when others are baptized after us, it is the once-for-all sacrament. The Eucharist, on the other hand, is a continual sacrament, one the church returns to again and again.

Meals are the settings in which families rehearse their stories, repeatedly trading tales and histories, realizing afresh what it means to be a Webber, a Clapp, or whomever. To be who you are you must remember who you were. Without memory there is no identity or vision and so no personhood. The Eucharist is the church's meal, a repast taken to praise God, to nourish it, and to refresh its memory and so its unique identity and its eschatological vision. The remembering of the Eucharist is of a high kind indeed: it is remembering that is more than memorial, but that makes the story that is remembered real and powerful for today. Like baptism, the Eucharist is participation in the story of Israel and Jesus. In a fragmented, dis-membered, rootless world, the church serves a crucial service in coming together for the Eucharist, learning to be a whole body, re-membering and rerooting its identity and its vision.

In its own way, the Eucharist enacts the span of the story of Israel and Christ. The bread of Eucharist recalls grain and the good creation from which it comes. Jesus' Last Supper was a Passover meal, signaling the pivotal event in Israel's history, the Exodus. The bread, of course, also symbolizes Christ's body, given up in death and resurrected in triumph over death. Wine is a natural biblical symbol for blood, since it is the color of blood and is called the "blood of grapes" (Gen. 49:11; Deut. 32:14). In addition, blood was considered the animating stuff of animals and humanity, making Christ's shedding of blood on creation's behalf all the more meaningful. Eating the bread (the body of Christ) and drinking the wine (the blood of Christ) are potent symbols of taking Christ's life into our life.

The Eucharist is preeminently a sacrament of joy and thanksgiving (hence its name, which translated literally means a "good gift"). It is laden with associations of the consummation's wedding feast of the Lamb and his people (Rev. 19; Mark 14:25). It is a celebration par excellence, and so the earliest church understood it (Acts 2:46–47). With the Eucharist at its center, the church can never forget it is a community of giftedness. In the Eucharist we are first of all given the gifts of creation and redemption. Our "acceptance of them commits us to living according to what may be called an ethic of gratitude."[18] It might be said that in partaking of the Eucharist we commit ourselves to living eucharistically. In the Eucharist we are given much, not only Christ, but also ourselves and one another, as Augustine so eloquently recognized in one of his sermons: "Since you are the Body of Christ and His members, it is the mystery of yourselves which lies upon the Lord's Table: it is the mystery of yourselves which you receive."[19]

Binding us together in gratitude, the Eucharist is the sacrament of unity. Once again we can see Paul's ethical concerns flowing naturally from the liturgy: "Because there is one loaf, we, many as we are, are one body; for it is one loaf of which we all partake" (1 Cor. 10:17). In his own way Paul appears to be saying, "You accepted the Eucharist, now live eucharistically."

The unity of the Eucharist stands over against the sad fragmentation of the world. Christians may dwell within nations that declare other peoples enemies, but in the Eucharist the American Christian is united with the Russian Christian, the Chinese with the Japanese, and so on. At this depth-political level, the Eucharist radically calls into question the conflicts between nations; the unity of the sacrament takes precedence, for the faithful Christian, over the unity of nationhood. In the words of Anglican writer A. G. Hebert, "God has created and established a unity for mankind, through Christ, to draw all men out of loneliness, isolation, and enmity with one another, into the fellowship of His universal Family, a fellowship which the Church exists to express."[20]

Of course, much of our current division is due to overweening special interests and privatism. The Eucharist is an enacted judgment on these things, especially when they arise within the church. So Paul is concerned that the Corinthian church eats and drinks with disregard of the poor. "It follows that anyone who eats the bread or drinks the cup of the Lord unworthily will be guilty of desecrating the body and blood of the Lord," he writes (1 Cor. 11:27). To practice the Eucharist is to experience dissonance between our real, uncaring disunity and the wholeness the Jesus story would lead us to embody. Thus it moves us on our way, perhaps with a shot of holy impatience.

The Eucharist carries its own energy and hope for healing and wholeness. However raggedly the church today embodies unity, the Eucharist has already been a powerful channel leading to that unity. Political enemies kneel at the altar and drink from the common cup. This hardly means an end to their anger and separateness, but it does mean they acknowledge a deeper level on which they would meet. People who sit down to eat together may at least ask each other to pass the salt, and with that simple request communication has begun. The Eucharist is such an occasion. When political opponents partake of the same loaf and cup, the church demonstrates to the world that there is an allegiance more important than politics.

More significantly, the Eucharist bears the promise of God's unity and wholeness. As we have emphasized, worship is fundamentally a response to what God has done, not to what humanity has done and can do. To partake of the Eucharist is to be stung by the brokenness of our community, but also to be salved by the expectation of a day when "On this mountain the Lord of Hosts will prepare a banquet of rich fare for all peoples, a banquet of wines well matured and richest fare. . . . On this mountain the Lord will swallow up that veil that shrouds all the people, the pall thrown over all the nations; he will swallow up death for ever. Then the Lord God will wipe away the tears from every face and remove the reproach of his people from the whole earth" (Isa. 25:6–8).

It is only such hope that emboldens the church to face a second dissonance: that between the fullness of the Eucharist and the physical hunger of so many on earth. The Eucharist is a sign of justice, a sign that the hungry are beckoned by God and that he wills an end to their hunger (Isa. 55:1; Luke 6:21). As Brian Wren writes in *The Christian Century*, "Jesus chose to share bread and wine in the context of the Passover," a time when the Israelites were present to the slavery of their ancestors, remembering the whiplashes and forced labor, and the miraculous release from the superpower Egypt. "It is all very earthy and material—a matter of politics, flesh and blood."[21]

From its dawning days, the church recognized that the Eucharist signaled something more than political and economic liberation, but never less. Like Paul, St. John Chrysostom drew a direct ethical line between the Eucharist and care for the poor:

Do you wish to honor the Body of Christ? Do not despise him when he is naked. Do not honor him here in the church building with silks, only to neglect him outside, when he is suffering from cold and from nakedness. For he who said, "This is my Body" is the same who said, "You saw man, a hungry man, and you did not give me to eat." Of what use is it to load the table of Christ? Feed the hungry and then come and decorate the table. You are making a golden chalice and you do not give a cup of cold water? The Temple of your afflicted brother's body is more precious than this Temple [the church building]. The Body of Christ becomes for you an altar. It is more holy than the altar of stone on which you celebrate the holy sacrifice. You are able to contemplate this altar everywhere, in the street and in the open squares.[22]

Chrysostom was considered a golden-tongued orator, but that

such words were not mere rhetoric is proved by Aristides, a pagan who defended Christians before the emperor Hadrian. Said Aristides, "Christians love one another. . . . If one of them is poor and there isn't enough food to go around, they fast several days to give him the food he needs. . . . This is really a new kind of person. There is something divine in them."[23]

The recovery of a vigorous connection between the Eucharist and hunger (or rather the elimination of hunger) is all the more sharply needed in an age when "hunger is no longer necessary." In the words of Bread for the World's Art Simon, "Our technology would allow us to overcome the worst features of hunger and malnutrition within a generation *if there was the political willingness.* That is, we have the means to eliminate hunger, but not the determination."[24]

The Eucharist provides just such determination. It is, after all, bread and wine, not the unaltered creation of grain and grapes, that are consecrated at the altar at each celebration. This means that we bring our human labor, and with it the means of production, to the Eucharist. These things we offer up to God for his blessing, but not only for his blessing: what God would bless, he can also judge. We do a daring thing when we offer our work and fruit to God since, in truth, we offer not only our honest toil, but any dishonesty and injustice we have perpetrated or participated in: perhaps corners cut that make for an inferior product, the consumption of food produced through the exploitation of labor, or allowing sexual harassment in the workplace to continue unchecked; certainly our little but significant links in the political chain that acquiesces to unnecessary hunger in the world.

Not that the celebration of the Lord's Supper should be turned into a guilt trip. It is, after all, the Eucharist. But it can and should be an occasion to give up to God the best we can possibly offer, to pray, in expectant hope, that the fruits and labor we bring will increasingly be untainted by injustice. The Eucharist is the enjoyment of God's generosity. It is our faith-building response to the professed belief that he will provide, that he will give us our daily bread even after we have let go of political and economic practices that seemed to ensure our bread but not bread for others.

Once again worship leads us to a dangerous but exciting place, a place where calculation withers and imagination blooms. The

God we worship is never the one we think we control, one who yields to the comfortable predictability of our stingy, constricting expectations. If baptism requires that we let go, the Eucharist will not allow us to regain a tight grip. James Allen Sparks tells of a church that decorated its Communion table with a lacquered bread loaf. One Sunday, in the middle of a Communion service, a visiting preacher mistakenly "took the mummified bread with both hands" and blessed it. Suddenly, "Yielding to two hundred pounds of preacher, the crisp shell vaporized with a thunderous explosion before the startled assembly."[25]

The Eucharist, like God, is good—but not safe.

PART THREE
THE ENACTMENT OF STORY

The form of this world, distorted by sin, is passing away and we are taught that God is preparing a new dwelling and a new earth in which righteousness dwells. . . .

Far from diminishing our concern to develop this earth, the expectancy of a new earth should spur us on, for it is here that the body of a new human family grows, foreshadowing in some way the age which is to come.

—"PASTORAL CONSTITUTION ON THE CHURCH IN THE MODERN WORLD," *DOCUMENTS OF VATICAN II*

Introduction

We have been arguing that the church, when it is true to itself, is not tame. However, worship and church involvement are caricatured in our society as exactly that. And Christians have complied with the caricature. We have failed to understand our story and the identity that derives from it as something distinct from the wider culture. In the end, it is not the world that has made the church into a reflexive endorser of the status quo or, in other instances, a reflexive proponent of the latest socio-political revolution. The world has not made the church safe and predictable; the church has.

So it is the church that has a responsibility to stop seeing its worship as something inert and powerless. Worship shapes Christians into a people apart, a people living in ultimate contradiction to the world's fundamental operating principles. That is why worship is necessary and central. But, as we have also said, the church cannot stop with its worship. Christians do not do what they do on Sunday in isolation from what they do on Monday through Saturday. Worship itself is a witness to the world, but Christians do not complete the liturgy unless they are intentional about living out the effects of worship, of the Jesus story enacted. This they do when they leave the place of worship and go out "into" the world.

The church remains the church even when it is not gathered for worship. It is necessary for the church to gather, but it is not less necessary for it to disperse. In its gathering and dispersal, the church is like nuclear fusion. Nuclear energy is attained by concentrating and fusing atomic elements. There can be no explosion and release of power without fusion occurring first.

Similarly, in its public worship the church is concentrated or fused. It gains its power from gathering. But it gathers and fuses with the intention of exploding. Its explosion drives it beyond the walls of its worship and makes it a power to be reckoned with in the world. Atomic elements are transformed by their fusion. And likewise the church's explosion sends Christians into the world on a particular trajectory, as persons empowered and made distinctive by the unique fusion of their worship.

It is the aftermath of the explosion we want to consider in detail now. If worship is more than a bland exercise in private piety, what does it effect in the world, in the neighborhoods and jobs to which Christians disperse after they have gathered?

Worship relates to everything a Christian does—work, play, relationships, political involvement, and the rest. To explore the connection between worship and life beyond the church walls, we will in chapter 6 concentrate on the relationship of worship to the world in general and the impact worship can have on our view of life, time, and matter.

Christians also disperse to grapple with the great and critical issues of the day. The understanding of the church and its worship for which we have argued is irrelevant and even harmful unless it enables the church to confront and engage these critical concerns. Chapter 7, then, suggests what difference a truly diacritical Christian community can make in relation to several of the pressing social problems of the day.

6. Worship and Our Life in the World

It is genuinely hard for twentieth-century American Christians to believe they are doing anything important when they worship. Worship is a formality for many Christians on the Left; they suspect the truly significant Christian actions occur in a picket line or on Capitol Hill. Their temptation is to turn worship into a political rally, complete with a rousing (or sometimes guilt-inducing) sermon intended to jolt people into the fray over Nicaragua, or awaken them to "the" Christian imperative on homosexual rights.

Those Christians oriented toward the political Right are usually also more conservative in their theological convictions. Consequently, they may be less forward about playing down the importance of worship. Yet the tendency here, too, is to act as if the "real" Christian life happens elsewhere. In these circles there is little sense of the church as a people called. The gathered church ends up a kind of glorified civic club. Sunday morning is a time when individual Christians happen together for an hour or two of inspiration and encouragement for the week. It is a retreat from reality where one gets strength for the return to reality. With this understanding of worship, the religious Right is unable to see any relation between worship and the public life. In its more brazen moments, the Right can only be honest about its low evaluation of worship. As Tim LaHaye declared in late 1985, changing the nation's laws is now more important than bringing about a "spiritual revival."[1] Apparently LaHaye understands spirituality as private and legislation as public, with never the twain to meet.

In the end, it makes little difference whether worship is absorbed into sheer political activism and rendered no different from—and subordinate to—political and societal life, or whether it is not related to political and societal life at all. Either way, it is trivialized.

And yet worship—praise, proclamation, and the sacraments—is the one activity unique to the church. The secular Left and Right champion the same political causes that Christians inclined to the Left or Right champion. But the secular Left and Right do not hear, tell, and rehearse the story of Israel and Jesus Christ. Only the church does so. This is its single distinctive contribution to society. If the church fails to take worship seriously, it ironically forfeits its true gift to the world.

In the previous chapter we discussed the different elements of worship. In this chapter we intend to back away and view worship as a whole, trying to understand how and in what ways it is central to the existence of a true diacritical community in the world. In other words, why is worship central and how does that centrality affect the church's depth politics?

WHAT WORSHIP DOES

The term "liturgy" comes from two Greek works, *laos* and *ergon*, meaning "people" and "work." So liturgy is the work par excellence of the church. It is what the church does as the church—something that, if omitted, would mean the church was no longer the church.

In a fragmented America struggling for hope, searching for a story that pulls together all the shattered pieces, the church can do nothing more politically significant than remember and act out its story. Remembrance and enactment of the story is the essence of Christian worship. Far from being a retreat from the "real" world, worship enables Christians to see what the real world is and equips them to live in it. This is a crucial point, one we will return to later in this chapter.

Liturgy also implies mission. Students of the liturgy have noted that the word may mean not only work *of* the people but work *for* the people. In Roman society, "to build a bridge for a public road across a stream on one's private property would constitute a liturgy." Military service at one's own expense was an act of liturgy. The wealthy sought favor by sponsoring lavish "liturgies"—huge dramas for the entertainment of the citizenry.[2] Likewise, in its own liturgy, the church builds bridges at its expense and welcomes the world's crossing. If nothing else, the church hopes its own drama, the weekly liturgy, will introduce those who don't really know him to the God at the center of the drama.

So all worship is related to mission. The church exists for the sake of the world. It does not shape and strengthen its identity so that it can retreat into invulnerable isolation. Instead, it learns to live by the Jesus story so that others—the entire world, the church prays—will learn to live according to reality and wholeness. The people who are now the church are joyful that God has already invited them together, but they live in hope of a greater joy, a joy that achieves fullness only with the kingdom's fullness.

Finally, the liturgy itself demands that the church go out into the world. The Eastern Orthodox speak of mission as "liturgy after the liturgy."[3] What is meant by this expression is captured by the final words of the old Roman Mass, "*Ite missa est,*" meaning "Get out!" Until we have gotten out, the liturgy—the work of the church for the world—is not finished.

All this talk of "the liturgy" may create the impression that worship makes a difference only in the "high" or liturgical churches. But every church has a liturgy, and worship always shapes the way Christians see the world and proceed in mission. This is demonstrated in many communions, but perhaps nowhere more dramatically than one distinctly "nonliturgical" body, the black American church. We could find few better illustrations of our point that worship is central and from it grows the church's depth politics.

BLACK AMERICANS AND THE SIGNIFICANCE OF WORSHIP

Although, as we have noted, worship is often trivialized today, there is a sense in which it unfailingly resists trivialization. This is so because worship always—at least ostensibly—refers to God. The word "worship" springs from the archaic English "worthship," and when we worship we assign ultimate worth. Nothing exposes idolatry like true worship. When the Christian worships she is assigning ultimate worth to God and implicitly calling into question any part of her life that fails to put God above every other loyalty.

As early American slave traders and owners intuitively recognized, their worship judged their economic practice. In the antebellum South, Christian worship forcefully implied (even if most sermons did not declare it) that cotton was *not* king. And what if, slave owners correctly reasoned, the slaves took such implications to heart? But, of course the slaves did. Despite persistent efforts to tailor black worship to white advantage, the black church from then until now has been a source of spiritual and political power. It is no accident that many of the leaders of black America, from Nat Turner to Martin Luther King, Jr., have been preachers.

Theologian James Cone has written illuminatingly on the important role worship plays for black Americans.[4] Worship is the dynamic assurance that black people are not merely objects of oppression, as society has so often told them, but are objects of God's love and redemption. They may experience humiliation within the structures of white society six days a week, but they "gather together each Sunday morning in order to experience another definition of their humanity." Worship "produces a radical transformation in people's identity. The janitor becomes the chairperson of the Deacon Board; the maid becomes the president of Stewardess Board Number 1. Everybody becomes Mr. and Mrs., or Brother and Sister. The last becomes first, making a radical change of perception in one's self and one's calling in society."

This occurs because, in the black tradition, preaching basically is a matter of "telling God's story." Hearing God's story, a people who have been in bondage and therefore appreciate freedom respond passionately with songs and "shouts" (bodily movements). As Cone emphasizes, blacks "*have* church"—worship is active and involving, not a matter of spectating or detached listening to an intellectually brilliant lecture.

We mentioned in a previous chapter that the church is a body with its roots in the future and its branches in the present. This is certainly true of the black church, made up of persons who know oppression in the present but have faith that God will eventually consummate his kingdom. The congregation sings and shouts because, in worship, the future becomes present: "That is why it is hard to sit still in a black worship service," Cone says.

Yet worship, according to Cone, is not an excuse to escape difficult realities. Freed in worship, black Christians "struggle to realize in the society the freedom they experience in their worship life." Salvation, in other words, makes a difference here and now, in history. And it makes more of a difference by virtue of the fact that it extends beyond history, beyond death.

"If death is the ultimate power and life has no future beyond this world," Cone writes, "then the rulers of the state who control the military are in the place of God. They have the future in their hands, and the oppressed can be made to obey the law of injustice." But since "death has been conquered, we are truly free to be human in history, knowing that we have a 'home over yonder.' 'The home over yonder,' vividly and artistically described in the slave songs, is the gift of salvation granted in the resurrection of Jesus." That gift sustains the oppressed in the struggle for justice, energizing them so that they will not get tired or grow "afraid of the risks of freedom." They can have hope and confidence because "Jesus' resurrection already defines what the ultimate outcome will be."

The existence of the black church strikingly demonstrates that worship need be neither purely political or restricted to an exercise of private piety. It affirms worship as a passionate response to God's action in history. "He rebuked the Red Sea and it dried up, he led his people through the deeps as through the wilderness. . . . O praise the Lord" (Ps. 106:9,48). And "Worthy is the Lamb, the Lamb that was slain, to receive all power and wealth, wisdom and might, honor and glory and praise!" (Rev. 5:12). When blacks (and the rest of us) worship, the story of Israel and Jesus becomes our story. And when that story becomes our story, we see God above all else. In the words of Abraham Joshua Heschel, "Worship is a way of seeing the world in the light of God."[5] The black church gives us a glimpse of just how profoundly depth-political worship can be.

WORSHIP AND REALITY

A new and true vision is at the base of worship's depth-political power. To see the world in the light of God is to see the world as it really is—not as any nation-state, corporation, revolutionary movement, or other power would have us see it. So Christians are mistaken when they allow themselves to be intimidated by the insinuation that the church and worship have nothing to do with the "real world." God is at work, of course, in all of reality, and not merely in our fleeting hours of public worship. But humanity is a blinded race, and in worship we have a chance to look on the world in its "full, transparent reality—as the place of God's love and activity." Worship, as St. Leo the Great said, "makes conspicuous" the world as it is.[6] Christian worship is an exercise in vision, practice at seeing. God grants the church special sight (Eph. 1:17–18), and in worship Christians learn gradually to make use of this gift, like the newly sighted who "see men as trees walking" and at first proceed haltingly in a dazzling world of colors and dimensions. To understand better how the church learns to see, we need to consider the essence of worship: praise.

Sadly, "praise" is not a term easily associated with the daily grind of honest reality. In fact, the word seems to summarize the worst of the worship-as-withdrawal mentality. So-called praise music is the muzak of hymnody. And those who constantly speak of "praising the Lord" too often do so in the context of praising him for their continued material comfort and spiritual frivolity. Yet praise is nothing so insubstantial in the story of Israel and Jesus. The Psalms are praises lifted up in face of bloody battles, famines, the guilt of murder, and the shame of exile. The early Christians sang in prison and looked on fasting as a form of thanksgiving. Scriptural praise is not praise for famines and prison, but it is praise offered in and through the harshest circumstances of reality—primarily, of course, the cruel circumstance of the cross.

This is praise in its full and original sense, praise that will help us learn to see what is real. Biblical praise can be defined as the grateful acknowledgment of reality. As the opening phrase of the *Te Deum laudamus* states, "We praise thee, O God; we acknowledge thee to be the Lord." In this line praise is parallel to the acknowledgment that God is the Lord; his lordship is the ultimate reality. Consequently, praise is not as vapid and petty as the thoughtless overuse of the term might lead us to expect. In fact, it is aggressive. By praising God, we displace from the center of our attention and ambition all competing allegiances—personal, political, economic, or otherwise. Personally, we admit that our ego is not the pivot point of the universe. Politically, we set aside any political system's explicit or implicit claim that the future of the world depends on it. Economically, we disavow the assertion that material wealth and class standing constitute genuine riches.

True praise, then, immediately reveals false idols. In the ante-Nicene period, the church's baptismal liturgy included a moment in which the initiate looked west (whence comes the power of darkness) and spat in the face of the devil. Christians no longer literally expectorate during baptism, but the praise of God is a decisive spit at the overweening claims of the powers and principalities. To praise God is to reveal and renounce the illusion of consumerism, the mass media, or any other power—the illusion that we need it and cannot live well without it. As black worshipers have learned, the powers do not grant us our identity or define our vision. So praise is practice of depth politics.

On the level of depth politics, praise teaches that we can only live well by depending on God and his surprising gifts. Thus, when we earlier defined praise we did not define it simply as the acknowledgment of reality, but as the *grateful* acknowledgment of reality. As we indicated in chapter 5, reality as it is revealed in the story of Israel and Jesus shows that the church is a people called. It is a people called to a diacritical community, to live anchored in giftedness, eschatological vision, forgiven-ness, and presence. Here, then, is the indispensable importance of worship: in a fragmented and chaotic world, the church gains its identity by the act of praise, by celebrating the story of Israel and Jesus. In the confession of sin it begins to understand what it means to be a community of forgiven-ness. In preaching prophetic words it begins to understand what it means to be a diacritical community. In partaking of the sacraments it begins to understand what it is to be a community of presence. In thanksgiving it begins to understand what it means to be a community of giftedness. Performing these actions—these actions distinctive to it among all the institutions on earth—the church is most fully a community, and most fully a sign and light of true life to the world. For as T. S. Eliot asks,

> What life have you if you have not life together?
> There is no life that is not in community,
> And no community not lived in praise of GOD.[7]

WORSHIP AND THE REST OF LIFE

Praise, the *sine qua non* of worship, enables Christians to see the world in the light of God. But that conclusion, by itself, can still leave worship unconnected with life. It is in Monday through Saturday, after all, that we live most of our lives. In Monday through Saturday, we work, we play, we do our politics, and we build our society. It might be that Christians glimpse reality on Sunday, but how is that glimpse of reality carried into Monday through Saturday?

The short answer is this: the church learns to see every other day through Sunday. Monday through Saturday are included in Sunday. Public worship, writes theologian Leonel Mitchell, "does not sit alone and isolated from the day-to-day business of living, but permeates it and offers it all—joys, sorrows, successes, failure, frustrations, anger, and love—to God."[8]

The longer answer requires us to consider how all of reality is included and transformed in worship. The reality human beings inhabit consists of matter and time. Matter and time are included and transformed in worship; consequently, so are our lives, privately and politically. By transforming our matter and time, worship fosters a diacritical community, a potent depth-political presence.

MATTER AND DEPTH POLITICS

The God Christians worship is believed to be the creator and redeemer of the physical, material world. The Christ story, as we noted in chapter 3, has God creating the physical world and communicating his presence to the world through matter. Adam and Eve are given bodies and a garden. Just as a mother communicates her love to her child by feeding it—sustaining its life—God communicated his love to humanity by providing the food of the garden.

But matter is the vehicle for evil as well as good, and so the devil persuaded Eve to eat of the fruit of the forbidden tree. Later, humanity uses physical matter to build the blasphemous Tower of Babel. A possible divine response to the Fall would have been to abandon matter, since it has been perverted. In the story of Israel and Jesus, however, God does not abandon matter. He operates through and with it to create the people Israel, a light to the nations that he leads out of the *physical* nation of Egypt, across the *physical* Red Sea. Finally, in Jesus, God is incarnate, physically assuming the very matter that has been abused by humanity.

To use matter (water, wine, and bread) in worship is to make a depth-political affirmation. It affirms that the true meaning of the world cannot be grasped apart from the Judeo-Christian conviction that the world has been created. When the story of creation and re-creation through the work of Christ is rehearsed in worship, the worshiper's vision of the world is formed. The worshiping Christian begins to live from the perspective—a political perspective—that God owns the world. No tyrant or ideology can legitimately make a God-like claim on the created order. Creation belongs to Christ, not to the politically powerful.

Because God is the Lord of matter, Jews and Christians have always taken the material world seriously. They cannot abandon what God has not abandoned. Accordingly, the book of Exodus includes elaborate instructions for the construction of a tabernacle, indicating that material things belong to God and can be used to communicate truth about God. The recognition that the "glory of the Lord filled the tabernacle" (40:34) admits God's presence in a particular space. Later, Jesus is baptized in water, breaks bread, and consecrates wine. He uses the elements of matter (like his fellow Jews) to communicate the love and presence of God.

The use of matter to communicate God's presence is a sign that God, through the story of Israel and Jesus, liberated the material world from the principalities and powers. As Paul writes, the material world has been subjected to futility (Rom. 8:20). Thus the powers put matter to evil use: to fashion—from the created order—knives, bombs, and other implements of discord and violence. The wrong uses of creation distort and destroy life. They foster wars, warp minds, and destroy families.

But Paul also indicates that the created order will be set free (Rom. 8:21). Enacting the eschatological vision, liturgy frees matter to be used in redemptive ways. Wood, stone, mortar, bread, oil, and wine become symbols of the new order, the consummated kingdom under Christ. Matter is returned to its original purpose, to praise and serve God. Worship, then, strikes at the depth-political dimension of our labor: what we do with the matter God has given us.

In the offering the church gives its gifts back to God. Christians have worked through the week, using the bodies, talents, and material creation given them by a gracious God. On Sundays they bring their work into worship, offering up a portion of what this work has brought them. That offering represents the failures and the successes of their work; it means that all the dealings of the office and field are brought under the roof of the sanctuary. In turn, all these offerings will be distributed for the edification, the building up, of the body.

Worship, then, puts our labor in a depth-political context. In worship the fruit of our labor is grafted on to the tree of Jesus' story. Just as Jesus fed the multitude, we surrender our labor so that none may go hungry. Just as Jesus admitted that all good and life-giving things come from God, we let go of some assets to admit that we are dependent on the Father. Remembering Christ and expecting his return, we respond with gifts that make work meaningful.

The ethical implications are clear. As our labor is taken into the story of Jesus, it must conform more and more to that story. God expects our work to be consistent with our worship: "Will the Lord accept thousands of rams or ten thousand rivers of oil? Shall I offer my eldest son for my own wrongdoing, my children for my own sin? God has told you what is good; and what is it that the Lord asks of you? Only to act justly, to love loyalty, to walk wisely before our God" (Mic. 6:7–8). If we admit by our act of offering that these gifts come ultimately from God, how can we dare misuse them? How can our personal labor be dishonest or less than generous? How can we not be increasingly uncomfortable with economic practices that leave people hungry or unemployed? There is no escaping the social and political implications of worship.

TIME AND DEPTH POLITICS

If matter is brought into worship and placed beneath Christ's lordship, so is time. Greek philosophy tended toward an abstruse, highly theoretical understanding of time. Time (as bound to creation) was separated from timelessness or eternity (as above and beyond creation). Because of this separation, the Greeks could not envision the eternal entering time. Humanity was imprisoned within ultimately meaningless time. Time was cyclical, having no goal or destination.

Although elements of this philosophy of time influenced the New Testament, the story of Israel and Jesus presents a fundamentally different approach to time. For the Hebrews, God acted in physical time. The Old Testament gives significant attention to the precise time of Moses and the Exodus (see Deut. 1:9, 16, 18), to the reign of David (1 Chron. 21:28–29), and the building of Solomon's Temple (2 Chron. 7:8). God acted in time on behalf of Israel. Time was understood to have a destination (thus the importance of prophecy) and was organized around God's special acts in history. The yearly cycle included the festivals of Passover, the Feast of Weeks, the Feast of Tabernacles, and others, all arising from the works of God in Israel's story.

As it did with matter, Christianity adopted the Hebrew relation to time. Through Jesus, God acted in history to extend salvation to the Gentiles. In its worship, the church looks back through significant time: primarily to the life and death of Christ, but also to works of God in the history of Israel. Christian worship is also forward looking: it anticipates the return of Christ and consummation of the kingdom planted in Israel and brought to light in Christ. Worship orders time and gives it meaning within the story of Israel and Jesus.

Although the Christian day of worship is not strictly a Sabbath, it incorporates elements of the Sabbath. The Hebrew weekly cycle of time consists of six days' work and one day of rest. As philosopher Nicholas Wolterstorff points out, this alternation is "profoundly peculiar. It corresponds to no natural cycle at all." Other cultures have regularly gone longer periods without setting aside work. The work-rest cycle of Israel was not like a harvest festival, falling at a certain time due to the dictates of nature. "Instead," Wolterstorff observes, "this rhythm was given to be practiced as a remembrance, as a memorial of the pattern of God's creative activity and of the pattern of Israel's liberating experience."[9]

Consequently, all of life was ordered around worship. In Wolterstorff's words, "the very rhythm of everyday life was to be a liturgical practice."[10] Christians do the same. Our day set aside is Sunday, a pattern arising directly from the story of Jesus. Every Sunday is a little Easter, Resurrection Day, a feast day reminding us and making real and present to us the truth that Christ rose from the dead and is Lord of all things. Worship gives our work meaning by putting matter into a context; it also gives our work meaning by putting time into a context—the context of remembering and expecting Jesus. Worship renders time Christian.

Time shaped after the story of Jesus has depth-political implications. The ordering of time—and events made important within time—give meaning and context to all aspects of our lives. Every society orders time according to historic events and values it considers central to the society. In America, Independence Day celebrates the nation's beginning. Fireworks recall the war fought to decolonize America. Flagwaving and parades communicate the societal value of patriotism, a value rooted in and extending from July 4, 1776.

Societies also order time in commemoration of heroes whose character the society believes should be emulated. The birthdays of George Washington and Abraham Lincoln call to mind their legendary traits of honesty (young George admitting that he chopped down the cherry tree; Abe pursuing a customer two miles to return a few pennies). In Nicaragua, Augusto Sandino's birthday and memory represent the kind of courage, shrewdness, and tenacity Sandinistas believe their country needs. No matter where one lives, time is political.

Christian time relativizes all other orderings of time. This need not mean that Christians refuse to celebrate national holidays; it does mean their respective national holidays are subordinated and ordered under a wider and deeper scheme of time. Since the ordering of time rehearses a community's story, the church would surely have a stronger and more distinct identity if it paid closer attention to the ancient Christian calendar.

We can agree that the Reformers had reason to cut back the calendar: each day of the year had been named after a saint. Yet it may have been a mistake to eliminate the calendar completely. In a divided world, with many powers competing for its loyalty against its Lord, the church needs every help it can get to maintain its unique identity. The seasons of Advent, Christmas, Epiphany, Lent, Easter, and Pentecost allow the church to live into its story annually—from the birth of Christ to the coming of the Holy Spirit. They draw Christians back to the source of their identity and into a rehearsal of the characters they must have if they are to live their stories after the story of Christ.

Christmas is the birthday of the Prince of Peace, an occasion that, if celebrated after the biblically informed expectations of an Advent season, can serve to mold a people of peace. This people will undoubtedly include "just war" theorists as well as pacifists—but both will be reminded that Christians must seek ways to be a people of peace in a world of violence. Lent, to cite another season, is an exercise in joyful humility. What might this mean when practiced in a society inclined to insecure boasting about size and numbers—the "biggest" this, the "most" that?

The practice of the Christian year can check and correct orderings of time that pay no attention to the story of Israel and Jesus. It is not a time scheme invented to have political effects, but then Independence Day and May Day were not created for the express purpose of political effect. It simply has to do with the way humans are. Time matters. The calendar is unavoidably political. What people truly value can be easily determined by consulting their datebooks.

IN CONCLUSION: WORSHIP AND JUSTICE

Worship claims space and time for the Christian story. It is the regular practice of ordering things and events in the light of God, the ground of reality. On Sunday the church learns what it is to be Christian Monday through Saturday. This alone sets the community apart and sustains it in the differentness that is the hope of the world. Christians worship together so that their lives may become a living sacrifice, their identities and visions no longer adapted to the present world but transformed and made new (Rom. 12:1–2).

By ordering matter and time by the mandates of the kingdom, worship is an epiphany of justice. It proclaims the inevitability of the just kingdom, in which the powers will be vanquished and matter and time, the stuff of human life, will no longer be used as vehicles of oppression.

Furthermore, the liturgy calls the church to be an eschatological community, to live justly now. That the early Christians lived eschatologically is borne witness in the second-century *Letter to Diognetus*. The letter notes that the Christians "do not cast out their offspring." They "love all men," though they are "persecuted by all." They are poor, "and yet they make many rich."[11] That such a life was expected of Christians is borne out in another ancient document, *The Apostolic Tradition of Hippolytus*. The *Tradition* describes expectations of second- and third-century candidates for baptism, including the criteria that they "have honored the widows," visited the sick, and "been active in well-doing."[12]

A life of justice, lived in the wake of a new identity and vision, was expected—and that expectation was made clear in the liturgy itself. In such a way worship is depth political, critiquing and challenging the necessity of injustice in the world. But of course all governments—and most tyrants—claim to seek the establishment of justice. As a diacritical and eschatological community, the church is a check on the noble designs of nations and other powers that go astray and end up attempting to establish "justice" by unjust means. The church's worship relativizes all human attempts to manage history and create a world without justice, for the liturgy always points to the final, complete establishment of justice as a work of God, a work to which the eschatological community now witnesses—peaceably, justly, and noncoercively.

The church worships so that all of life, individual and social, may become worship. Worship grooms a people to think theologically and act doxologically. That is what Christians are called to do every day of the week and year, privately and publicly: to live in mind of God's kingdom, with unceasing praise.

7. The Church and Current Social Issues

In 1857, the Dutch Reformed Church (DRC) of South Africa made a fateful decision. In deference to the "weaknesses of some," the DRC synod allowed the Lord's Supper to be celebrated in separate services for church members of different races. The ideology of apartheid—with its roots scandalously embedded in the church—grew steadily following this liturgical alteration.[1] Today apartheid stands as bitter proof that the church, as a community, can radically affect the surrounding society and that a church's worship has consequences for the kind of church it will become.

In 1982, the Dutch Reformed Mission Church, the "colored" contingent of the DRC's "family of churches," recognized such to be the case. Apartheid, in the Mission Church's judgment, was an institutionalized denial of the faith. The Mission Church declared itself in the midst of a *status confessionis*, a decisive "moment of truth" when the gospel itself is at stake and confession of it must be clearly made. The result was the Belhar Confession, so called because it was formulated in Belhar, Cape Town. The confession is remarkable in many respects, but we wish here to draw attention to three.[2]

First, *the Belhar Confession recognizes the importance of witness by a body of Christians (the church) and not simply individual Christians operating more or less independently.* The confession opens by affirming trust in "the triune God, Father, Son, and Holy Spirit, who gathers, protects, and cares for his Church by his Word and Spirit." It moves rapidly to profess belief that in the church "Christ's work of reconciliation is made manifest." Accordingly, the church is "called to be the salt of the earth and the light of the world." It is "witness both by word and by deed to the new heaven and the new earth in which righteousness dwells."

Note the affirmation that the church as a body is gathered by

God and essential to the witness of the gospel. As a commentator on the confession observes, "If the church should neglect to sound the demands of the kingdom farther than just the heart of the individual, it forsakes its calling as witness and community to the kingdom. A church which concerns itself only with individual salvation while society in general denies and opposes Christ's kingship is in reality not enhancing the gospel message but impeding it."[3]

Second, *the Belhar Confession stresses that the church is distinct from the world and must resolutely oppose the principalities and powers wherever they manifest themselves.* "God by his life-giving Word and Spirit has conquered the powers of sin and death," the confession proclaims. The church's witness to the defeat of the powers includes its demonstration, as a reconciled people, that hatred and enmity are not final. Such a witness "can open new possibilities of life for society and the world." This means, another commentator on the confession writes, that "no structure is without its injustice, no society without its poor and no civil order without evil. . . . If the congregation is to continue its critical witness against the powers that be, then it must not be subservient to any political or social order. It must jealously keep vigil over its independence."[4]

Third, and finally, *the Belhar Confession takes note of the significance of the church's worship.* It affirms that Christians "are baptized with one baptism, eat of one bread and drink of one cup, confess one name." Again we allow a South African commentator to draw out the implications of the confession: Worship "is an act in which the congregation again anchors itself in the entire Word of God and sets itself up against the world and against false belief. And it is a bond which binds it to the fellowship of believers, affirming the baptismal vows."[5]

We dwell on the Belhar Confession here because the church that makes it, a people of the truth in a desperate land, is a living embodiment of what we have proposed. It is a church that recognizes the centrality of its community under God, understanding that the church must be a unique presence in the world and that the church is shaped by the distinctive story it learns and rehearses in worship. In other words, the Dutch Reformed Mission Church realizes that its primary task is simply to be the church. This in itself will have a tremendous depth-political effect, opening "new possibilities of life for society and the world."

Any hope for the healing of South Africa surely lies with those empowered by a faith and perspective like that of the Mission Church. By comparison the United States is a less inflamed country, but it too is divided and uncomfortably close to national panic. What difference can such a perspective make here?

Using the perspective we have developed thus far—that the church is a diacritical community shaped and empowered by the story it practices in worship—we want to examine six social and moral issues. Each of the issues touches on debates central to the nation's identity. Each of them is divisive and contributes to the country's fragmentation. We have space for only the most cursory discussion of the issues. Our intention in taking up these profound problems is certainly not to pretend we can solve them. (Indeed, we recognize that some in the church will disagree with the basic position we take on each of these issues.) We hope only to concretely indicate that the church, exactly by being the church, can contribute distinctively and tellingly to the society's political good.

PORNOGRAPHY

Pornography has long been an important issue to conservative Christians. With the 1986 Meese Commission Report, the recent protest of feminists, and the increasing degradation of "hard" pornography, it is an item on the national agenda.

Working from its own Scripture and tradition, the church has clear reasons to oppose pornography. But it is part of a pluralistic society, in which many citizens do not consider the same Scripture and tradition authoritative. Debate tends to magnetize, by now rather predictably, around what the law should and should not do about pornography. Any progress is high-centered on arguments over civil liberties and alleged censorship. Given unfortunate antisexual episodes in Christian history and the current climate of wide sexual freedom, it is all too easy for proponents of pornography (or at least of the freedom to distribute it) to paint the Christians who oppose them as repressed "Puritans" who want to impose their narrow-minded morality on everyone else.

Strategically, then, Christians who work against pornography would be wise to ask themselves what they can do to keep from playing into the hands of those who want few if any strictures on the publication of pornography. They might first observe that law is largely coercive, enforced by duress and threat of penalty. Of course, law is not entirely negative: it serves to uphold a society's minimal ideals. Laws that make sense and seem justifiable to most citizens are not perceived to be coercive so much as protective and laudatory. But when debate over an issue rages and law is proposed as the answer, it is law's coercive element that opponents will most loudly protest.

Consequently, Christians who fight pornography primarily by emphasizing the law's role meet with formidable opposition. The coercive element of law is immediately called to the fore and Christians pushing the law are easily pictured as intolerant bedroom invaders. Soon enough many are embroiled in complicated (and often specious) arguments about how "Christian" America was or was not, and should or should not be. But what if the same Christians did not start with the law? Might they get the debate off high-center by first clearing the terrain for their position?

That is, pornography may be more effectively curtailed by beginning with the church rather than the nation and with witness rather than coercion. As a diacritical community, the church will not only oppose pornography and chide pornographers; it will demonstrate an alternative to the attitudes and practices that make pornography attractive and possible. Such a shift in ground has the effect of undercutting three essential assumptions of the pro-pornography forces—three assumptions, incidentally, too readily shared by many other Americans.

The first assumption is an overemphasized fixation on the value of individualism and private choice. These are indeed important values, ones that the church itself strongly supports. But to fixate on individual choice is to forget that every individual is a part of a society and that individual choices affect society. The conventional wisdom is that every individual should be allowed to do whatever he or she pleases, as long as no one is hurt in the process. This fixation has allowed pornographers to argue, with perceived cogency, that pornography is harmless. At least in "legitimate" pornography, models are not "forced" to pose for pictures, and no one is "forced" to buy pornographic literature. Pornography may or may not be unhealthy for those who read it—experts testify on either side—so whose right is it to stop it from being distributed?

The second assumption undergirding arguments made by pornographers is the essential innocence of consumerism. Unless obvious harm is occurring, this argument runs, the free market should be left alone. Capitalism is an economic system with no faults we're willing to admit. Sometimes it is abused, but there is nothing intrinsic to it that contributes to social problems.

And the third assumption is that sexuality is merely a recreational practice. Sex is for fun and enjoyment, first and foremost. In many ways, choosing a sexual partner or a sexual practice is like choosing what game to play for the evening. Poker? Chess? Bridge? It makes little difference so long as everyone enjoys it.

How might the church respond diacritically to these three widespread assumptions?

First, it might submit (by word and the example of its practice) that human beings are not atomistic individuals. We all look to communities for our physical and spiritual sustenance. Pornography is not simply a matter of private choice; it involves an entire network of photographers, models, writers, editors, advertisers, distributors, and consumers. And much pornography is antisocial: "It tears away at bonds that hold a society together. Societies are clearly made healthy by a sense of trust and respect, which recognizes a shared worth or value in all persons."[6] Pornography encourages the consumer to view the model as (at best) an object of impersonal lust or (at worst) of fantasized violence. By embodying mutual trust, help, and delight, the church can stand as a living repudiation of the notion that people are best off by trying to deny their need for community and will make questionable the assumption that antisocial pornography is harmless to society's health.

Second, the church might challenge head-on the country's wholehearted trust in capitalistic consumerism. Pornography, after all, is not merely a matter of private lust. Economics make participation in the production of pornography alluring, especially to those who have few alternatives for gainful employment. Consumerism facilitates an understanding of pornographic models as simple objects of consumption, centering the consumer on his own enjoyment and encouraging no thought about what his consumption means to others. The church, on the other hand, can never view persons as mere objects of consumption. It believes (in the memorable phrase of C. S. Lewis) that, "Next to the Blessed Sacrament, your neighbour is the holiest object presented to your senses."[7] Taking this approach as a basic operating principle of its ethics, it will contradict any economic mechanics that tend to dehumanize persons.

Third, the church might challenge the assumption that sex is merely recreational. It understands sex as enjoyable, certainly, but also as a mystery that cannot be trivialized to the level of simple hedonism. Sex has to do with life itself, drawing closer together a man and a woman who have made lifelong commitments, making possible the creation of new persons with all their unimaginable promise. Games grow tiresome. If the church embodies a sexuality that is playful but more than a game, wider society will naturally question its own assumptions about a sexual practice that appears shallow and monotonous in comparison.

Of course, we are speaking of an imperfect church in an imperfect world. The church will never be a sterling example of these counterassumptions, and the world will never be easily persuaded the counterassumptions are true. The legal battle will remain necessary and will remain a battle. But to the degree the church takes note of underlying societal notions and successfully contradicts them in word and deed, to that degree antipornography laws (and the enforcement of those already in effect) will be sensible and appealing to wider society.

AIDS AND HOMOSEXUALITY

Are diseases simply random viruses and bacteria, a matter of indifferent infection or the mechanical degeneration of organs? Essayist Susan Sontag has compellingly demonstrated that human diseases are much more: they are also social constructions. As social creatures, we respond not only to the objective disease of the sick person; we respond to what our society tells us the illness *means*. Diseases we can understand and that are not fatal are rarely accompanied by moral judgment. Thus leprosy, once mysterious and incurable, was regarded as a judgment of God. Today its causes are understood and it can be controlled; it is no longer considered judgment.

Similarly, cardiac disease, which is straightforward if not entirely curable, is not as repugnant as cancer. Because we do not know exactly what causes cancer and because it is so often terminal, the cancer patient is felt to be threatening. Contact with the cancer sufferer "inevitably feels like trespass; worse, the violation of a taboo."[8] To contract cancer can jeopardize one's love life, one's chance for a promotion, or even one's job. The 1966 Freedom of Information Act cited "treatment for cancer" in a clause exempting from disclosure material the revelation of which "would be an unwarranted invasion of personal privacy."[9]

Sontag's conclusion: "Any disease that is treated as a mystery and acutely enough feared will be felt to be morally, if not literally, contagious."[10] If ever a disease qualified for this category, surely it is AIDS (Acquired Immune Deficiency Syndrome). In addition to being a mystery and acutely feared, AIDS is frequently transmitted by the morally charged actions of sexual practice. Homosexuals suffering from the disease are widely believed to deserve it and at the same time abhorred for the threat "they" have introduced to the straight population.

Much of the church's response to the crisis has fed this attitude, in cases going so far as to proclaim that AIDS is God's judgment on homosexuals. Whatever else may be said about this attitude, it is self-contradictory. On the one hand (when homosexuals are afflicted), AIDS is considered the just judgment of God. But on the other hand (when heterosexuals are afflicted), AIDS is not judgment—it is nothing more than the scientifically unexplainable breakdown of the body's immune systems. Because heterosexuals will increasingly suffer AIDS, we can expect the "just judgment" theory to die out over the next several years. Will the church replace it with a more adequate (not to mention compassionate) social construct?

Three broad options have surfaced for responding to AIDS. The first is quarantine. But 1.5 million persons are already infected, and the disease is known not to be transmitted by ordinary, nonsexual contact. Quarantine is morally repugnant and impractical. The second suggested option is to identify AIDS carriers to the rest of the population, with some pundits all too seriously recommending tattoos. This response is Orwellian, and the last society to implement such tactics was Nazi Germany. The third option is to eliminate (or at least minimize) behaviors that spread the virus—cut back on promiscuous, unprotected sex; educate drug users about the dangers of dirty needles.

Surely the last of these options is the one most amenable to the church. It is not immoral or frighteningly coercive, and it jibes with the church's traditional sexual commitments. Promoting education and "safe sex": this much the church should do with the rest of society. But it can do more.

It can, for starters, recognize that AIDS will continue to be widely understood as the "gay plague" for the foreseeable future. Consequently a response to AIDS realistically requires fresh scrutiny of the church's response to homosexuals and to the societal preoccupation with sex in general.

This requires, first of all, that the church admit its own responsibility for the development of the homosexual subculture. The church, more so than society in general, has responded to the homosexual with overbearing rejection and hostility. This has left homosexuals—social creatures no less than heterosexuals—with a single alternative: the gay subculture. As an anonymous writer in the *National Review* put it, "A heterosexual can be straight anywhere, but a homosexual can be *safely* gay only in a gay environment."[11] If the church learns, albeit in the smallest ways, to give the homosexual a home, there will be less incentive to flee to a community dominated by those who have learned (not without reason) to hate the story of Jesus. A start, in these unfortunate times, is surely to attend to AIDS sufferers with the promises of the gospel *and* abiding, patient presence. To simply make a hit-and-run presentation of the gospel promises is a travesty of the gospel itself. And to be present without speaking the gospel is to fail in providing our unique and most valuable gift.

The real tension, of course, comes here: how can the church extend genuine care and friendship to homosexuals and, simultaneously, not condone homosexual practice? The usual answer is that the church must "accept the sinner while condemning the sin," which entails that the homosexual will be expected to give up his sexual practice. Understandably, this rings hollow to many (perhaps most) homosexuals. After all, the church itself has been preaching the sex act (albeit among married heterosexuals) as among the highest and holiest pleasures available to humankind. How would anyone dare to do without it? We would suggest the church's recommendation of celibacy is more likely to ring true if two things happen.

The first is what has already been discussed. If persons who happen to be homosexuals sense a genuine and persistent concern for their persons (whatever their sexual practices), they are more likely to take seriously our claim that giving up homosexual sex is the will of a loving, noncapricious God.

Second is the witness of the church's single heterosexuals. It is they who can live out a celibate but fulfilled existence (supported, let us hope, by married Christians who do not act as if the celibates are missing some essential, far superior experience). It is they who can convincingly remind homosexuals (and everyone else) that if sex were the key to health and happiness, prostitutes and philanderers would be the healthiest and happiest people on earth. All of this is not to say that sex, rightfully understood, is anything less than wonderful or good. (In fact it is so good it does not have to be propped up by denigrating any other good, and celibacy is one of those goods.) It is to say that the church often forgets the fullness of the story it lives by, a fullness including the possibility that singleness can be transformed into a way of life that can vitally serve the kingdom. In such a context, living without sex begins to be something imaginable—and even commendable.

We should conclude with a reminder that AIDS is not a "gay disease." It plagues straights as well, leaving no room for heterosexual complacency. A saner, nonpromiscuous approach to sexuality will benefit heterosexuals no less than homosexuals. One profound sign of our society's brokenness is its attitudes toward sexuality. AIDS and other issues indicate that the church need not so much address separate issues of the moment as live out organically whole and healthy sexual relationships. Only this will address the deeper, more profound confusions of value that underlie pornography, AIDS, promiscuity—and priggish, body-fearing Christian piety as well.

ABORTION

Of the many issues dividing American society today, abortion is broadly regarded as the most divisive. Like pornography, the debate over abortion now centers on the law, and both prolife and prochoice campaigners see absolutely essential principles at stake. In their own ways, both sides consider the outcome a matter of life and death. By now the arguments have grown old, but there seems to be little substantive change in the issue—abortions continue apace and protestors show no signs of retiring. What distinctive contribution can the church make?

It might begin, once again, by recognizing that the legal battle is not the entire war. Law is certainly an essential factor in the battle. Some 1.5 million abortions occur annually (4,000 daily). With the steep increase in the number of abortions since 1973 (the year of the Supreme Court's *Roe* v. *Wade* ruling), few would hold the law has nothing to do with the rapid increase of the practice. Surely a change in the law would decrease the number of abortions.

Yet there is serious reason to believe it would fall woefully short of satisfactorily braking abortion-on-demand. The country is now in its second decade of legal, permissible abortion. Swayed by the implied endorsement of law and the acceptance of the culture, wide swaths of the population are persuaded abortion-on-demand is quite justifiable. Abortion is now conspicuously available, and technical developments have made it a brief and relatively safe procedure. It is no longer a matter of sneaking into dark back alleys and suffering the coathanger ministrations of an ill-informed opportunist.

Abruptly and simply rendering the procedure illegal, then, would probably result in widespread flouting of the law and a possible rise in organized crime (not unlike the results of Prohibition). Theologian James Burtchaell estimates that at least 500,000 abortions would still be obtained annually.[12] This would be a two-thirds reduction—a significant feat—but would leave an unacceptable number of fetuses unprotected and society in a state of profound conflict. What is needed is not merely a shift in law, but a change in the national character.

The truth is that we have become a society in which human offspring are eliminated as casually as tonsils. Only a small fraction of abortions occur to protect the mother's physical health or to terminate a pregnancy resulting from a crime. As a community of truth, the church can unrelentingly press home the reality of this fact. It can pose the penetrating questions: why this many abortions? And is the indiscriminate practice of abortion enhancing our social or individual lives?

Two important aspects underlie the spiraling incidence of abortion. The first is an exaggeration of the necessity of private choice. By this logic, abortion-on-demand is ultimately a matter for the pregnant woman and her alone. The abortion laws as they stand isolate a woman from her boyfriend or husband, a daughter from her parents. They do little to encourage trust and the mutual confrontation of difficult decisions. And we cannot glibly and insensitively imply that abortions sought under such conditions are merely matters of "convenience" for the woman. Too often pregnant women find themselves abandoned. Ours is not a society well prepared to assist single mothers, as the rising rate of impoverished women and children demonstrates.

A second factor boosting abortion's acceptability is discussed in Kristin Luker's *Abortion and the Politics of Motherhood*.[13] Sociologist Luker surveyed prolife and prochoice activists, learning that they have diametrically opposed understandings of suffering. The prochoice people expected life to be basically free of unwanted burdens. The prolifers, on the other hand, believed some hardship is inevitable. The attitude of the prochoice camp is probably more widespread in America. Bathed in affluence and surrounded by impressive medical technology, in our heart of hearts we believe all suffering is to be avoided and can be avoided.

The church, a diacritical community, answers to a story that challenges both of these assumptions. Although wider society does not subscribe to its story, the church can present, in the society's vocabulary, aspects of reality the church's story suggests.

Deeply aware of its status as a community, of humans created as social beings, and of redemption that will culminate in a *city*, the church can persistently question: is abortion not a societal matter? Is it not mass culture, after all, in hundreds of television programs, films, and newspaper stories, that persuades individuals indiscriminate abortion is okay? Does society really have no interest in a practice that contributes substantially to a decline in the renewal of its population?

Looking to its own story, the church also doubts the cultural assumption that suffering is mostly avoidable and that no good ever comes from suffering. It looks to the people of Israel, who fled suffering in Egypt but learned in the wilderness that liberation, too, entails hardship. It follows a Savior who in the same breath promises ultimate liberation and the pain of a cross. It can ask: is all suffering really avoidable? Do unending attempts to avoid it sometimes result in greater suffering? Do not the things we value most—relationships, fulfilling jobs, advanced education—require considerable sacrifice? If we lose our absolute abhorrence of immediate suffering, can we not look further at the alternatives to abortion and imagine richer, more lasting rewards arising from them?

The church will most effectively alter attitudes about abortion on demand not simply by posing questions, but by making those questions thinkable with its life. Let it be clear that women who choose abortion usually do not do so lightly, but only after agonizing and searching their souls, finally deciding that abortion is the most ethical option for them in their situation. So the church must not simply confront individual "sinners." It must confront the wounded values of a society that leaves pregnant women to confront woeful choices all alone. It must be a community that affirms our dependency on one another and our willingness, even at personal cost, to support another who has chosen a difficult alternative. It must be a practicing community of forgiven-ness, a community that will suffer hardship without, in turn, inflicting violence on the unborn. Finally, the church must be a sign of a people who accept the unexpected and do not avoid it when it costs something. It must witness to a vision that can see suffering pregnant (sometimes literally) with hope. Accordingly, and only accordingly, it can embrace children as the strangers they are, realizing that "children exist to destroy hopes . . . and then to replace them with enhanced hopes."[14]

THE POOR

Debates about America's welfare programs are as old as the programs themselves. Underlying all the debates are differing attitudes toward the poor. Jesus said the poor would always be with us; he might have added that bitter disagreement about the poor would always be with us as well. The church can offer no special insight into what particular public and/or private aid will best assist the poor. Instead, it can best affect this issue by discerning, then living out the implications of its story for the poor, doing so in diacritical relation to society's underlying attitudes.

We have already suggested, in Chapter 3, that the kingdom inaugurated by Christ takes special account of parenthetical people—not least those faced with oppression and economic deprivation. From beginning to end, the Bible presents a story of a God inclined to favor and help those who cannot help themselves. He leads a poor and powerless people out of Egypt; through the prophets he consistently pleads the case of the widow, the orphan, and the homeless; in Jesus he came to us as a poor and homeless man, announcing the kingdom to the poor and keeping company with the poor. It is not simply diehard social gospelers, but thoroughly orthodox theologians such as Abraham Kuyper who have recognized, "When rich and poor stand opposed to each other, [Jesus] never takes His place with the wealthier, but always stands with the poorer."[15]

But does an "option for the poor" mean that God chooses one class of people and rejects another? Does it mean that the gospel is, at core, no more than an inspiration for economic redistribution? Does it mean there is some special (and saving) merit to the degradation of poverty? Clearly a positive answer to any or all of these queries will lead into an inescapable thicket of difficulties. So how is the church to understand the Christian story's unsettling attention to the poor and embody that story so that the poor will be genuinely helped and the world truthfully confronted?

As Karl Barth suggests, we do best to see that concern for the poor is tied directly to the logic of the gospel. Ultimately the church cares for the poor because any other political attitude "rejects the divine justification."[16] If the story of Israel and Christ discloses reality, it shows that we are all poor and wretched before God. Evangelical theologian Carl F. H. Henry is exactly right to assert,

The prime requisite for authentic reading of Scripture is that I see *myself* as impoverished (indeed, as the poorest of the poor), and that I see Jesus Christ as the only "just and holy One," the Suffering Servant who made my sins his own and who volunteers new moral life and power to do His will. *My own* spiritual poverty must be faced if I am really to grasp the full plight of others, for without the redemptive riches of Christ no hope exists for any of us.[17]

The world desires to ignore the poor, to put them out of sight and out of mind, because they witness to an unwelcome truth: we are all impoverished. Inasmuch as we are self-made, we are self-made paupers and cripples. In the laughter, might, and righteousness of the wealthy, the world's "mortal wound is concealed. But it is brought to light in the misery of those who suffer."[18]

Understanding as much, the church sees the poor as a special clue to reality, to the truth that we are all poor and God cares for the poor. Therefore the church is hospitable to the poor, to promise that comes disguised as a stranger in need. In gratitude and in correspondence to the revealed character of God, the church can only respond with its own special concern for the poor. By committing itself to justice and care for the destitute, who knows what the church will learn of God's mercy?

But the world's aversion to admitting its poverty and need is profound. Seeking to deny it, the world is inclined to rob the economically poor of their dignity. And the robbing of dignity knows no political monopoly: dignity can be taken by the conservative who insists the poor are slothful and deserving of poverty or by the liberal who enjoys moral superiority because of his welfare projects. If the poor can be blamed or merely pitied for their misery, the world can keep intact its illusion that it, unlike the reprehensible or pitiful poor, can take care of itself—that it does not need God.

The church's witness is just the opposite. Justice and true charity are concerns of those who have begun to understand reality, who find courage in Christ to admit their own neediness. Thus the church insists on the dignity of the poor, for dignity is a gift of God given to all and earned by none. It is urgently concerned that society not oppress the poor and that it does what it can to alleviate the suffering of those remaining impoverished. Yet the church cannot simply be satisfied with the impersonal, bureaucratic assistance of the state. As Jesus professed, human needs exceed bread and water. Providing food and medical care for the poor is certainly necessary for their dignity, but it is not sufficient. In the words of philosopher Michael Ignatieff,

It is the manner of giving that counts and the moral basis on which it is given: whether [impoverished] strangers at my door get their stories listened to by the social worker, whether the ambulance man takes care not to jostle them when they are taken down the steep stairs of their apartment building, whether a nurse sits with them in the hospital when they are frightened and alone. Respect and dignity are conferred by gestures such as these. They are gestures too much a matter of human art to be made a consistent matter of administrative routine.[19]

Since this is so, the church cannot deny the poor or ostracize them by leaving them to the detached ministrations of overloaded social workers. Rather, it chooses, in its Eucharist, to *eat* with the poor. Its worship is a rehearsal of Jesus' meal-communion with the poor of his day. To fail in welcoming the poor to the Eucharist is to divide the community, desecrate the Supper, and invite the judgment of God (1 Cor. 11:18–29).

So the church's worship is its most significant action on behalf of the poor. In its worship it learns its identity, the kind of community it must be, and practices being that kind of community. It sees the reality of its own poverty and is given the courage to admit it and, in admitting it, to become a people that invites the (economically) poor into its presence. For finally it realizes: "How can Christians and Christian churches bear witness to [their] God if they do not struggle with the admittedly difficult task of becoming an *unnatural* community in which poor and rich, powerful insiders and powerless outsiders, live in fellowship with each other? If we are not willing to risk popularity and numerical growth to become such a community, how can we bear witness to the Christ who not only went out to the poor and outcast but invited them to come in to him, who not only sought out their company but welcomed them into his company . . . ?"[20]

DRUGS

The American drug menace is advanced enough to gain the nation's attention, perhaps to a degree it hasn't since before Prohibition. And well it should gain such attention. Narcotics traffic in the United States is estimated at between $27 billion and $110 billion.[21] Drugs directly damage or destroy millions of individual

Americans, but they also damage society. Besides the effects on families and costs in the workplace, drug traffic breeds violence. Not only is the government tempted to break out heavy weaponry—city streets become war zones, with young children serving as "scouts" and "runners" for teenage dealers.

Four prominent solutions to the narcotization of the nation have been proposed. First, stop the import of illegal drugs with interdiction and border patrols. Second, make more arrests, more convictions, and more severe penalties (possibly including capital punishment) for drug dealers. Third, implement urine and other tests (saliva and even hair can be sampled for evidence of drug use) to pressure drug users in the marketplace, government, and athletic arena. And fourth, educate children to say no to drugs.

Some of these proposals have more merit than others, but all fail to cut below the surface of the problem, for marijuana, heroin, cocaine, and other contraband are not the only or even the predominant drugs in use in America. There are approximately 100,000 deaths due directly to alcohol each year, 300,000 caused by the use of tobacco.[22] With so many casualties, the "War on Drugs" may be more literally a war than the rhetoric intends—considering that "only" 292,000 Americans died in World War II.

There appears to be a mentality encouraging drug use in general, even among those who use no illicit drugs (or, to narrow it further, who refuse alcohol and tobacco as well as the illegal drugs: there remains prodigious consumption of caffeine and Valium, for instance). President Nixon may have put pressure on Turkey and Mexico to stop drug traffic, and President Reagan sent troops to Bolivia. But how will armies outside our borders solve the problem if it is inside our borders, inside ourselves? Will stiffer enforcement and penalties stop an appreciable number of drug dealers when we continue to want drugs badly enough to make those who dare to deal extremely wealthy? Is drug testing morally acceptable? What will it do to employer-labor relations if implemented? And will all members of the population (including bosses, for instance) be tested? Will teaching children to say no be effective if societal example and insinuation continue to say yes, yes, yes?

If we are to hope for more than a short-lived abatement of (some) drug use, we must look deeper and determine why drugs of all sorts are so attractive to us. Drugs may be so attractive to us because they are enormously powerful. Alcohol does make us feel good. Caffeine wakes us up. With drugs we can eliminate polio; correct a life-threatening heart condition; remove the excruciating pain of a toothache; banish headaches, diarrhea, and dandruff; stop the plagues that once devastated entire continents—the list seems to go on and on. And that is precisely the problem.

Certainly many drugs are a boon to humanity, eliminating or reducing untold suffering. But we are apparently so taken with potent, quick, painless solutions to so many problems that we lose sight of the very real limitations of drugs. Indeed, powerful as drugs are, it is not only a matter of drugs. Technological innovations of all sorts have given us unprecedented comfort, convenience, and amusement. In every way, we are spoiled to expect instant and intense gratification. So even those not intoxicated by alcohol or marijuana are intoxicated by technological prowess. Our longing for an external "quick fix" to the drug problem is ironically a manifestation of the same attitude that makes drug use prevalent in our society.

The magical force we associate with even the most innocent of drugs shows up in their names: "vitamins" (literally, "vital amines") or "biogenic amines" (literally, "life-giving amines"). When the wonder drug cortisone was introduced, one observer said the reaction at medical conferences "more closely resembled [that at] revivalist meetings."[23] William James saw fit to include alcohol among his varieties of religious experience (for attempts to achieve a mystical sense of unity with basic reality); and a decidedly lesser light, Timothy Leary, promoted LSD as a "sacrament."[24] To repeat: drugs are terrifically powerful, and the expectations they engender are enhanced and reinforced by the advantages of technology.

But despite all this, the implacable fact remains. No drug or technological innovation can assuage loneliness, mend a broken heart, eliminate ennui, or still the longings of the human soul. However fervently we would wish to deny it, a good deal of suffering remains inevitable to our lot. The most potent (and especially illicit) drugs trade on illusion, the illusion that a pill or a shot or a drink can put us in touch with the creative power of the universe, make us better people, or simply make us forget how hard are the blows life can deal.

The church serves best, then, by recalling itself and its society to reality. It is a community committed to truth, a collection of people who worship to see the world as it really is and then go out and live according to the vision gained. In short, we might say the church is a community prepared, patient, and supported.

It is *prepared* to suffer because it is committed to living cruciformly, after the pattern of the cross. This does not mean the church seeks pain or calls its people to bear preventable anguish. It means the cross reveals the profound extent of the world's brokenness, a brokenness so extreme that only a suffering Savior could rescue it. To alleviate the suffering of others requires first that we not deny or flee from it. And to hear the gospel read and preached, to be baptized into Jesus' death, to drink in remembrance of his shed blood—all this is to practice facing the cross-pain that stands at the center of reality and redeems its otherwise absurd hurting.

The church is *patient* because, fortunately, there is more to its story and worship than the blood-stained, empty cross. There is the empty tomb of Easter. This, too, is heard in the gospel read, preached (good news!), and celebrated in the Eucharist. Nor does baptism end with our death in Christ, but with co-resurrection in Christ. In all of this we remember and re-present the resurrection: Christ's triumph over death and death's child, pain. We learn to anticipate an end to all suffering and strife, and the anticipation with which we are gifted is every bit as realistic as the admission of suffering and strife that now continues unabated.

Finally, the church is *supported*. Its liturgy is a practice of God's presence. He comes to be with us repeatedly, and we steadily acquire the skill of detecting grace in the most unexpected and unlikely circumstances. Primarily, we see it in the lives of others who are also looking for it. Because we are grace-bearers one to another, we are supported by one another in the difficult task of living without illusion in a brutal and broken world.

If the church is prepared, patient, and supported, it can exist without abusing drugs and without the mentality that encourages abuse.

NUCLEAR ARMS

A single fact hangs always in the consciousness or subconsciousness of modern men and women. The nuclear arms race is barely abating, and every second hostilities continue there looms the possibility of catastrophic attack, whether intentional or accidental. Perhaps no symbol grips the contemporary imagination so much as the mushroom cloud.

The cloud is a symbol of an ending: *the* ending. Its potency as a symbol testifies to the importance of endings. The truth of the matter is that we need endings. New Year's Eve parties, funerals, divorces, graduation ceremonies, retirement fetes—all are manifestations of the human need to punctuate and recognize endings. No story makes sense without an ending, no adventure without a destination, no undertaking without a goal. In the words of A. E. Harvey, "Unless we postulate an end towards which our efforts are tending, or which will relieve us from our suffering, our life becomes meaningless and even unendurable."[25]

But of course secular humanity, its expectation of a humanly constructed utopia by now severely shaken, is threatened exactly with the meaninglessness and unendurability of human history without an ending. Is nuclear weaponry an attempt to invent an ending or at least to hold in human hands the power of an ending? Certainly it was originally conceived as a radical effort to control human destiny. "Mark me well," a U.S. senator addressed his colleagues in 1951, "massive atomic deterring power can win us years of grace, years in which to wrench history from its present course and direct it toward the enshrinement of human brotherhood."[26]

What happens when the dream of "the enshrinement of human brotherhood" goes sour? Can those who have claimed the power of an ending easily relinquish it? Essayists on suicide have noted that suicide can be interpreted as an assertion of control over destiny or nature. Wrote Frenchman Antonin Artaud, "If I commit suicide, it will not be to destroy myself but to put myself back together again. . . . By suicide, I reintroduce my design in nature, I shall for the first time give things the shape of my will."[27] And before him Schopenhauer similarly observed, "Suicide may also be regarded as an experiment—a question which man puts to Nature, trying to force her to answer."[28] Perhaps, in some dark and perverted fashion, the continued buildup of nuclear armaments is the social equivalent of the despairing individual who keeps a bottle of pills in the drawer or a loaded revolver next to the bed. However bad things get, no matter how senseless they become, he is reassured that he at least possesses the power to end it all.

The dominant story of our time is that nuclear arms are the fate of the world. In them resides the power to stave off doomsday, so that we may work toward—what? The "enshrinement of human brotherhood"? If that now seems ridiculous or simply impossible, then the bomb spells the end. It is the reassurance that the absurdity of one damned thing after another will not go on forever.

A most regrettable thing is this: so potent is its ending that many Christians believe the story of the bomb. But it is emphatically not the Christian story. Nuclear armament is an object of idolatry, for the church is properly motivated by the fear of the Lord rather than the fear of the bomb.

Once again we witness the utter cruciality of the church's ability to stand in diacritical relation to the world. Without a true ending, the ending the church discards if its imagination is possessed by the bomb, the world has no alternative. It can only resort to its own, self-manufactured ending.

Thus the church can best face the nuclear crisis by being what it is: in this instance, an eschatological community. An eschatological community is one that always has its eyes on the end. And the end it has its eyes on is Jesus Christ, the alpha and the omega. In Christ, the gospel teaches, the end is determined—in a sense it has arrived. For those who live after the death and resurrection of Christ, "the end of the ages has come" (1 Cor. 10:11, RSV). At the cross the powers of sin and death were defeated, their age was ended, and at the consummation of this new age they will be vanquished forever.

The challenge of the church is to live in the light of this ending, the true ending of the world. In its worship, in baptism and the Eucharist, it practices the skill of living in that light.

At baptism it rehearses Christ's death, which "was and is the end of the world, the end of world history."[29] It remembers the vital truth that Christians are "baptized into his death" (Rom. 6:3). Each act of baptism sets aside every power and principality and therefore dislodges the bomb from its idolatrous grip on the church's imagination. Baptism frees the church to reclaim its rightful identity and see with its rightful eyes, and so to resist the identity of those who live in fear of the bomb and are blinded to any ending other than the bomb's. Of course wider society will not adopt the ending to which the church witnesses—at least not fully. But it will be challenged with the possibility of an alternative ending, and that alone is a ray of light cast across the bomb's all-encompassing shadow. Like the Marxists who freely admit they owe their future orientation to the Jesus story, society may adopt its own elements and construct for itself a new, more hopeful ending.

What skills to live free of idolatry does the church practice in the Eucharist? This, it will be remembered, is the sacrament of unity. Of it all Christians partake—Americans, British, French, Russians, Chinese, and the rest—and in it all Christians are made one with another, members of Christ's Body. The Eucharist is a rehearsal of peace. Whether pacifists or "just war" theorists, all Christians have a bias against violence and war.[30] The Eucharist is the implicit rebuking of any tendency to set national allegiance above allegiance to Christ. It is the embodied profession of our trust that individual and social identities rest in Christ and not in nation-states.

In addition, the bread and wine are gifts of the Lord that are not grasped and aggressively taken but received and accepted with open hands. They are sign-gifts that all of life is to be so received, the church's grateful admission that it is a people praying to live out of control, to leave history's outcome to God. Once again wider society's imagination is aroused: an alternative to human control at any cost is made thinkable. And the bomb loses a little bit more of its terrible luster.

CONCLUSION

In each of these brief "case studies" we have attempted to indicate how the church, by focusing on its distinctive identity and vision, can be a depth-political presence of great consequence to society. The church's calling, we believe, is not to change society as such, but to be a steady and true witness to Christ's inauguration of the kingdom and his victory over the powers. The greatest service the church can do society—always, but certainly in an era of fragmentation—is to live out its distinctive story, to be a diacritical community, to present the promising contradiction personified by Jesus the Nazarene. If grace is real, if the gospel is truth, that is enough and more than enough.

Notes

Chapter 1: The Centrality of the Church

1. Robert N. Bellah et al., *Habits of the Heart* (Berkeley and Los Angeles, CA: University of California Press, 1985), 65.
2. Ibid., 234.
3. Ibid., 227.
4. The metaphor is borrowed from Richard F. Lovelace, *Dynamics of Spiritual Life* (Downers Grove, IL: Inter-Varsity Press, 1979), 168.
5. Bellah, *Habits of the Heart*, 228.
6. Ibid., 232.
7. William Bole, "Religious Right 'Coming Out Party' Is Political Action Rally," *Religious News Service Special Report* (October 18, 1985): 8–10.
8. Karl Barth, *Church Dogmatics*, II/2, trans. G. W. Bromiley et al. (Edinburgh: Clark, 1957), 239, 264.
9. Adapted from a definition of "political activity" in Thomas H. Groome, *Christian Religious Education* (San Francisco: Harper & Row, 1980), 15.
10. Peter L. Berger, *Invitation to Sociology* (Garden City, New York: Doubleday, 1963), 130.
11. Stanley Hauerwas, *Truthfulness and Tragedy* (South Bend, IN: University of Notre Dame Press, 1977), 140.
12. George A. Lindbeck, *The Nature of Doctrine* (Philadelphia: Westminster, 1984), 133.
13. Ibid., 132.
14. Ibid., 127.

Part Two: Introduction

1. Phillip Moffitt, "The Power of One Woman," *Esquire* (January 1985): 11–12.
2. James W. McClendon, Jr., *Ethics* (Nashville, TN: Abingdon, 1986), 172.
3. Flannery O'Connor, *Mystery and Manners* (New York: Farrar, Straus and Giroux, 1969), 104.
4. Ibid., 192.
5. Reynolds Price, *The Palpable God* (San Francisco: North Point Press, 1985), 34.
6. Quoted in O'Connor, *Mystery and Manners*, 80.
7. H. Richard Niebuhr, *The Meaning of Revelation* (New York: Macmillan, 1941), 34.
8. John Howard Yoder, "The Use of the Bible in Theology," in Robert Johnson, ed., *The Use of the Bible in Theology: Evangelical Options* (Atlanta, GA: Knox, 1985), 120.

Chapter 2: The Politics of Evil

1. Karl Barth, *Dogmatics in Outline*, trans. G. T. Thomson (New York: Harper & Row, 1959), 54.
2. See James M. Houston, *I Believe in the Creator* (Grand Rapids, MI: Eerdmans, 1980), 79–80.

3. John Calvin, *The Epistle of Paul the Apostle to the Hebrews and the First and Second Epistles of St. Peter*, trans. William B. Johnston (Grand Rapids, MI: Eerdmans, 1963), 160.

4. M. Scott Peck, *The People of the Lie* (New York: Simon and Schuster, 1983), 207.

5. Richard J. Mouw, *Politics and the Biblical Drama* (Grand Rapids, MI: Baker, 1976), 32.

6. Thomas N. Finger, *Christian Theology* (Nashville, TN: Nelson, 1985), 328.

7. G. B. Caird, *Principalities and Powers* (London: Oxford Press, 1956), 6–7.

8. Hendrik Berkhof, *Christ and the Powers*, trans. John Howard Yoder (Scottdale, PA: Herald, 1977), 29.

9. See John Howard Yoder, *The Politics of Jesus* (Grand Rapids, MI: Eerdmans, 1972), 146.

10. Bernard Ramm, *Offense to Reason* (San Francisco: Harper & Row, 1985), 102–105.

11. See Gregor T. Goethals, *The TV Ritual: Worship at the Video Altar* (Boston: Beacon, 1981).

12. Jerry Mander, *Four Arguments for the Elimination of Television* (New York: Morrow Quill, 1978), 269.

13. Quoted in Peter G. Horsfield, *Religious Television* (New York: Longman, 1984), 70.

14. Virginia Stem Owens, *The Total Image* (Grand Rapids, MI: Eerdmans, 1980), 8.

15. Jacques Ellul, *The Political Illusion* (New York: Knopf, 1967), 186.

16. Saul Bellow, *Henderson the Rain King* (Harmondsworth, Middlesex, England: Penguin, 1966), 78.

17. Quoted in Dale Vree, *From Berkeley to East Berlin and Back* (Nashville, TN: Nelson, 1985), 105.

18. Pat Robertson, quoted in Horsfield, *Religious Television*, 72.

19. Ellul, *Political Illusion*, 16. That politicization and consumerism call us to different roles does not mean that one or the other is not a true power. Sometimes different powers are in accord, sometimes they are not: the ultimate aim of all fallen powers is chaos and destruction.

20. James W. McClendon, Jr., *Ethics* (Nashville, TN: Abingdon, 1986), 176.

21. Karl Barth, *The Christian Life*, trans. Geoffrey W. Bromiley (Grand Rapids, MI: Eerdmans, 1981), 216.

22. Kenneth Leech, *The Social God* (London: Sheldon, 1981), 52.

Chapter 3: Jesus and Depth Politics

1. Annie Dillard, *Pilgrim at Tinker Creek* (New York: Bantam, 1975), 29.

2. Søren Kierkegaard, *Training in Christianity*, trans. Walter Lowrie (Princeton, NJ: Princeton University Press, 1941), 44.

3. See Allen Verhey, *The Great Reversal* (Grand Rapids, MI: Eerdmans, 1984), 27–33.

4. Ernest Becker, *The Denial of Death* (New York: Free Press, 1973), 15.

5. Ibid., 12.

6. Ibid.

7. Ibid., 55–56.

8. G. B. Caird, *Principalities and Powers* (London: Oxford Press, 1956), p. 92.

9. The concept of living "out of control" comes from Stanley Hauerwas, *The Peaceable Kingdom* (Notre Dame, IN: University of Notre Dame Press, 1983), 105–106.

10. C. Rene Padilla, *Mission Between the Times* (Grand Rapids, MI: Eerdmans, 1985), 24.
11. George Eldon Ladd, *The Presence of the Future* (Grand Rapids, MI: Eerdmans, 1974), xi, 139.
12. See Verhey, *Great Reversal*, 74, and John Howard Yoder, *The Politics of Jesus* (Grand Rapids, MI: Eerdmans, 1972), 34, 240.
13. Padilla, *Mission Between the Times*, 23.
14. John Dominic Crossan, *The Dark Interval* (Allen, TX: Argus, 1975), 56.
15. Ibid., 108.
16. Ibid., 121–22.
17. David Rhoads and Donald Michie, *Mark as Story* (Philadelphia: Fortress, 1982), 77.
18. Ladd, *Presence of the Future*, 334.
19. On the treatment of women in first-century Palestine, see Joachim Jeremias, *Jerusalem in the Time of Jesus*, trans. F. H. and C. H. Cave (Philadelphia: Fortress, 1969), 359–76.
20. James R. Edwards, "The Strange Embraces of Jesus," *Christianity Today* (March 16, 1984): 26. On the status of children in the Greek and Roman cultures, see John Sommerville, *The Rise and Fall of Childhood* (Beverly Hills, CA: Sage, 1982), 48.
21. Walter Brueggemann, *The Prophetic Imagination* (Philadelphia: Fortress, 1978), 88.
22. Ibid., 83.
23. Verhey, *Great Reversal*, 30.
24. Ladd, *Presence of the Future*, 141, 204, 123.
25. Dorothy L. Sayers, *The Mind of the Maker* (San Francisco: Harper & Row, 1941), 188.

Chapter 4: The Church as Depth-Political Community

1. Gerhard Lohfink, *Jesus and Community*, trans. John P. Galvin (Philadelphia: Fortress, 1984), 9–10.
2. Paul D. Hanson, *The People Called* (San Francisco: Harper & Row, 1986), 428.
3. John Driver, *Understanding the Atonement for the Mission of the Church* (Scottdale, PA: Herald, 1986), 241.
4. Christopher J. H. Wright, *An Eye for an Eye* (Downers Grove, IL: Inter-Varsity, 1983), 198.
5. Lohfink, *Jesus and Community*, 62. For a suggestive exploration of what a more vital Christian community might have meant for Dietrich Bonhoeffer's famous dilemma (eventuating in his involvement in a plot to assassinate Hitler), see James W. McClendon, Jr., *Ethics* (Nashville, TN: Abingdon, 1986), 187–208.
6. As cited by William H. Willimon, *What's Right with the Church* (San Francisco: Harper & Row, 1985), 31.
7. Karl Barth, *Church Dogmatics*, IV/3.2, trans. G. W. Bromiley (Edinburgh: Clark, 1962), 779.
8. See John Howard Yoder, *The Priestly Kingdom* (Notre Dame, IN: University of Notre Dame Press, 1984), 174–75.
9. Peter Berger, "American Religion: Conservative Upsurge and Liberal Prospects," in Robert S. Michaelson and Wade Clark Roof, eds., *Liberal Protestantism* (New York: Pilgrim, 1986), 35.
10. Hanson writes, "Ethical behavior is thus Christ-like behavior, always focusing on the building up of the whole body of Christ, always motivated by concern for the weaker brother or sister" (*The People Called*, 447).

11. Karl Barth, *Church Dogmatics*, IV/1, trans. G. W. Bromiley (Edinburgh: Clark, 1956), 665.
12. See John D. Zizoulas, *Being as Communion* (Crestwood, NY: St. Vladimir's Seminary Press, 1985), 59.
13. This stimulating reading of the postresurrection accounts comes from Rowan Williams, *Resurrection* (New York: Pilgrim, 1984), 83.
14. Ibid., 77.
15. Ibid., 84.
16. The phrase comes from Williams, *Resurrection*, 52–75.
17. Hanson, *The People Called*, 447.
18. This sentence is adapted from a sentence in Douglas John Hall, "Beyond Cynicism and Credulity: On the Meaning of Christian Hope," *Princeton Seminary Bulletin*, vol. 6, no. 3 (1985): 201–10. The theme of our last three paragraphs is dependent on Hall's article.
19. Wright, *Eye for an Eye*, 135–36. See also Gerhard von Rad, *Old Testament Theology*, vol. 1, trans. D. M. G. Stalker (New York: Harper & Row, 1962), 371–72.
20. Eugene H. Peterson, *Traveling Light* (Downers Grove, IL: Inter-Varsity Press, 1982), 182.
21. Mary Gordon, *Final Payments* (New York: Random House, 1978), 130–31, 185.
22. "The General Thanksgiving," *Book of Common Prayer* (New York: Seabury, 1978), 101.
23. Peter Brown, *The World of Late Antiquity: A.D. 150–750* (New York: Harcourt, Brace, Jovanovich, 1971), 65, 68. In another place Brown comments, "Now it cannot be stressed often enough that the rise of Christianity in the third and fourth centuries was not merely the spread of certain doctrines in a society that already possessed its own principles of organization—as might well be the case in modern Africa; it was an effort of, often, rootless men to create a society in miniature, a 'people of God'; its appeal lay in its exceptional degree of cohesion" (*Religion and Society in the Age of St. Augustine* [New York: Harper & Row, 1972], 136).

Chapter 5: Worship and Depth Politics

1. Austin P. Flannery, ed., *Documents of Vatican II*, "The Constitution on the Sacred Liturgy," 10 (Grand Rapids, MI: Eerdmans, 1975), 6.
2. See Aidan Kavanagh, *On Liturgical Theology* (New York: Pueblo, 1984), 73–179.
3. Annie Dillard, *Teaching a Stone to Talk* (New York: Harper & Row, 1982), 40.
4. V. Gilbert Beers, Kenneth Kantzer, and David Wells, "Hard Questions for Robert Schuller About Sin and Self-Esteem," *Christianity Today* (August 10, 1984):16.
5. Walker Percy, *The Message in the Bottle* (New York: Farrar, Straus and Giroux, 1975), 119–49.
6. William H. Willimon, *The Service of God* (Nashville, TN: Abingdon, 1983), 154.
7. George Higgins, cited in Walter Burghardt, S.J., "Preaching the Just World," in Mark Searle, ed., *Liturgy and Social Justice* (Collegeville, MI: Liturgical Press, 1980), 49–50.
8. Willimon, *Service of God*, 154.
9. Cited in Urban Holmes, *Ministry and Imagination* (New York: Seabury, 1981), 109.
10. For this and further comment on baptism's symbols, see Mircea Eliade, *The*

Sacred and the Profane (New York: Harcourt, Brace and World, 1959), 129–36.
11. See Willimon, *Service of God*, 102.
12. See Charles P. Price and Louis Weil, *Liturgy for Living* (New York: Seabury, 1979), 99.
13. Aidan Kavanagh, *Made, Not Born* (Notre Dame, IN: University of Notre Dame Press, 1977), 3.
14. John H. Westerhoff, III, and William H. Willimon, *Liturgy and Learning Through the Life Cycle* (New York: Seabury, 1980), 11.
15. See Geoffrey Wainwright, *Doxology* (New York: Oxford University Press, 1980), 73–74.
16. Willimon, *Service of God*, 110.
17. Garrison Keillor, *Lake Wobegon Days* (New York: Viking, 1985), 207–8.
18. Wainwright, *Doxology*, 78.
19. Cited in A. G. Hebert, *Liturgy and Society* (London: Faber and Faber, 1935), 79.
20. Hebert, *Liturgy and Society*, 148–49.
21. Brian Wren, "Justice and Liberation in the Eucharist," *The Christian Century* (October 1, 1986):839–42.
22. Quoted in Tissa Balasuriya, *The Eucharist and Human Liberation* (Maryknoll, NY: Orbis, 1979), 26–27.
23. Quoted in Balasuriya, *Eucharist and Human Liberation*, 26 (italics deleted).
24. Barbara R. Thompson, " 'Hunger Is No Longer Necessary,' " an interview with Art Simon, *Christianity Today* (September 6, 1985):19.
25. Cited in "Reflections," *Christianity Today* (April 4, 1986):55.

Chapter 6: Worship and Our Life in the World

1. William Bole, "Religious Right 'Coming Out Party' Is Political Action Rally," *Religious News Service Special Report* (October 18, 1985):
2. Charles P. Price and Louis Weil, *Liturgy for Living* (New York: Seabury, 1979), 21.
3. Ion Bria, ed., *Go Forth in Peace* (Geneva: World Council of Churches Mission Series, 1986), 38–46.
4. James H. Cone, "Sanctification, Liberation, and Black Worship," *Theology Today* 35 (1978–79): 139–52.
5. Abraham Joshua Heschel, *I Asked for Wonder*, ed. Samuel H. Dresner (New York: Crossroad, 1983), 20.
6. William H. Willimon, *The Service of God* (Nashville, TN: Abingdon, 1983), 52.
7. T. S. Eliot, "Choruses From 'The Rock,' " in *Collected Poems* (New York: Harcourt, Brace and World, 1970), 154.
8. Leonel L. Mitchell, *Prayer Shapes Believing* (Minneapolis, MN: Winston, 1985), 7.
9. Nicholas Wolterstorff, *Until Justice and Peace Embrace* (Grand Rapids, MI: Eerdmans, 1983), 154.
10. Ibid. (italics deleted).
11. Cyril Richardson, ed., *Early Christian Fathers* (New York: Macmillan, 1970), 216–18.
12. *The Apostolic Tradition of Hippolytus*, trans. Burton Scott Easton (Cambridge: Archon, 1934), 44.

Chapter 7: The Church and Current Social Issues

1. G. D. Cloete and D. J. Smit, eds., *A Moment of Truth* (Grand Rapids, MI: Eerdmans, 1984), vii.

2. See Cloete and Smit, eds., *A Moment of Truth*, 1–4, for the complete text of the confession.

3. P. J. Robinson, "The 1982 Belhar Confession in Missionary Perspective," in Cloete and Smit, eds., *A Moment of Truth*, 47–48.

4. G. Bam, "Concerning Confession in the Local Church," in Cloete and Smit, eds., *A Moment of Truth*, 113–14.

5. Ibid., 106.

6. Stephen Monsma, "Should Christians Push Their Views on Others" in Tom Minnery, ed., *Pornography: A Human Tragedy* (Wheaton, IL: Tyndale, 1986), 80.

7. C. S. Lewis, *The Weight of Glory* (New York: Macmillan, 1965), 19.

8. Susan Sontag, *Illness as Metaphor* (New York: Farrar, Straus and Giroux, 1978), 6.

9. Cited in Sontag, *Illness as Metaphor*, 8.

10. Ibid., 6.

11. Anonymous, "A Conservative Speaks Out for Gay Rights," *National Review* (September 12, 1986): 30.

12. James Tunstead Burtchaell, "The Inability of Law to Accomplish Its Own Purposes: Reflections on the Abortion Debate," address delivered at the Americans United for Life Legal Defense Fund Forum, October 19, 1986, p. 22.

13. Kristin Luker, *Abortion and the Politics of Motherhood* (Berkeley and Los Angeles, CA: University of California Press, 1984).

14. Burtchaell, "The Inability of the Law," 26.

15. Cited in Nicholas Wolterstorff, *Until Justice and Peace Embrace* (Grand Rapids, MI: Eerdmans, 1983), 73.

16. Karl Barth, *Church Dogmatics*, II/1, trans. T. H. L. Parker et al. (Edinburgh: Clark, 1957), 387.

17. Carl F. H. Henry, "An Evangelical Appraisal of Liberation Theology," *This World*, no. 15 (Fall, 1986): 99–107.

18. Karl Barth, *Church Dogmatics*, IV/2, trans. G. W. Bromiley (Edinburgh: Clark, 1958), 191.

19. Michael Ignatieff, *The Needs of Strangers* (New York: Penguin, 1984), 16.

20. Shirley C. Guthrie, Jr., *Diversity in Faith—Unity in Christ* (Philadelphia: Westminster, 1986), 103.

21. Evan Thomas, "America's Crusade," *Time* (September 15, 1986): 63.

22. Ibid., 64.

23. Oliver Sacks, *Awakenings* (Garden City, NY: Doubleday, 1979), 22.

24. Ibid., 23.

25. A. E. Harvey, *Jesus and the Constraints of History* (Philadelphia: Westminster, 1982), 74.

26. Cited in Robert Jay Lifton and Nicholas Humphrey, eds., *In a Dark Time* (Cambridge, MA: Harvard University Press, 1984), 65.

27. Cited in Lifton and Humphrey, eds., *In a Dark Time*, 58.

28. Ibid.

29. Arthur C. Cochrane, *The Mystery of Peace* (Elgin, IL: Brethren Press, 1986), 83.

30. Richard B. Miller summarizes this frequently noted similarity between pacifism and the "just war" theory. Then, by probing surface differences between the two stances, he arrives at other significant, basic commonalities. See his "Christian Pacifism and Just-War Tenets: How Do They Diverge?" *Theological Studies* 47 (1986):448–72.

The Books Behind This Book:
For Further Reading

All authors hope their books are read and appreciated, but in an environment awash with as many books as ours that hope seems increasingly utopian. Just the same, we have an even more outlandish hope for this book: not only that it will be read, but that readers will find what it says important enough that they will push on and read some of the books that underlie what we have said and carry the discussion along further. Our ultimate hope is that American Christians will begin to think and act differently about their relation to the church and the church's relation to wider society. For the intrepid readers who have made it this far, then, we offer these suggestions for forging ahead.

Reading the signs of the times is never easy, but Americans at present are blessed with a growing number of thinkers who are watching and listening with great discernment. Premier among those who are helping us to see the causes of the national inability to agree on everything from welfare programs to abortion is Alasdair MacIntyre. His *After Virtue* (Notre Dame, IN: University of Notre Dame Press, 1981), already a classic, points to the necessity of communities bound together by a life-enhancing narrative—especially during what MacIntyre calls these "new dark ages." Robert Bellah and his sociologist colleagues in *Habits of the Heart* (Berkeley and Los Angeles, CA: University of California Press, 1985) build on MacIntyre's thesis and demonstrate the corrosive effects of extreme individualism.

For the effects of individualism in molding (warping?) evangelical theology and social engagement, we recommend Dennis P. Hollinger's *Individualism and Social Ethics* (Lanham, MD: University Press of America, 1983). And for a readable disentanglement of political, cultural conservatism from atomistic, laissez-faire economics, consult George F. Will's *Statecraft as Soulcraft* (New York: Simon and Schuster, 1983). Finally, to read the signs of these times no one can escape grappling with the issue of how church and state were originally related in our nation's history. There are dozens of titles already on the subject; one we find especially illuminating is *The First Liberty*, by William Lee Miller (New York: Alfred A. Knopf, 1985).

Believing it holds special promise for the dilemmas of the present moment, we have not hidden our enthusiasm for narrative theology. Anyone who wants to get a better idea about those dilemmas can look to all the authors we have mentioned above, and also to George A. Lindbeck. His *The Nature of Doctrine* (Philadelphia: Westminster, 1984) dissects the theological crisis of authority and indicates how narrative theology may help solve it. For those who remain leery of the entire idea that narrative is basic to Christian being, knowing, and doing, we recommend H. Richard Niebuhr's *The Meaning of Revelation* (New York: MacMillan, 1941), especially chapter 2. Michael Goldberg's *Theology and Narrative* (Nashville, TN: Abingdon, 1981) is the best introduction to narrative theology. Also helpful are *The Promise of Narrative Theology*, by George W. Stroup (Atlanta: John Knox, 1981) and *Story Theology*, by Terrence W. Tilley (Wilmington, DE: Michael Glazier, 1985).

Of course, much more important than the general theory of narrative theology is what shapes a particular narrative theology. We have argued that the primary shaping influence should be Scripture. Inspiring and challenging us all along has been the work of Stanley Hauerwas. Few other contemporary theologians are as committed to thinking biblically and creatively, on behalf of the church and for the sake of its mission in the world. The best introduction to Hauerwas is his *The Peaceable Kingdom* (Notre Dame, IN: University of Notre Dame Press, 1983). More readable and accessible is *Vision and Virtue* (Notre Dame, IN: University of Notre Dame Press, 1974), and most pertinent to this book's subject is *A Community of Character* (Notre Dame, IN: University of Notre Dame Press, 1981).

Tilling faithfully in the same vineyard as Hauerwas is James W. McClendon, Jr. His *Ethics* (Nashville, TN: Abingdon, 1986) eloquently demonstrates the power of a narrative-based, church-centered social ethic; with biographical sections on Jonathan Edwards, Dietrich Bonhoeffer, and Dorothy Day, it is also probably the most purely enjoyable systematic theology we've ever read.

Hauerwas and McClendon are both indebted to the Mennonite theologian John Howard Yoder. Almost singlehandedly, Yoder has caused the theological world to take seriously the Anabaptist ecclesiology and social ethic. All of his books demonstrate a devotion to reckoning with Scripture no matter how costly a discipleship it may entail and an equally rigorous intellect at work. Most relevant to the subject of our book is Yoder's *The Priestly Kingdom* (Notre Dame, IN: University of Notre Dame Press, 1984). Most accessible is his *The Original Revolution* (Scottdale, PA: Herald, 1971). Perhaps most influential is *The Politics of Jesus* (Grand Rapids, MI: Eerdmans, 1972).

Unfortunately, many will find Yoder's and Hauerwas's writing rather dense and difficult. So we wish to recommend Charles Scriven's *The Transformation of Culture* (Scottdale, PA: Herald, 1988), which engages H. Richard Niebuhr's *Christ and Culture* from an Anabaptist perspective. The thought of Yoder and Hauerwas are excellently and understandably presented by Scriven.

Our understanding of the church and its mission owes much to the writers we have just mentioned, but there are many other important sources. We have benefited from the teachings of the early church fathers. A handy compendium of their thoughts on the church is Thomas Halton's book *The Church* (Wilmington, DE: Michael Glazier, 1985). An excellent history of the doctrine of the church is Eric G. Jay's *The Church* (Atlanta: John Knox, 1978). Contemporary and provocative is Avery Dulles's *Models of the Church* (Garden City, NY: Doubleday, 1978). And it is always spiritually and intellectually salutary to comb Karl Barth's *Church Dogmatics* (trans. G. W. Bromiley; Edinburgh: Clark, 1956, 1958, 1961, 1962) consulting biblical references as you go. Volume four, parts one through three discuss the church in the most detail.

The aspect of our book that may strike some readers as most odd is our emphasis on the effects of worship far beyond the walls of church buildings. Worship has been grossly distorted in a society so enamored with "felt needs" that church leaders have traded away their rich gospel resources for the language and techniques of marketing. Robert Webber has devoted enormous

energy to the recovery of genuine Christian worship, working initially among evangelicals but increasingly in the mainline denominations as well. Now exactly ten years old, his first book, *Common
Roots* (Grand Rapids, MI: Zondervan, 1978) remains a fine introduction to the centrality of worship in the life of the church and
individual Christians. His *Worship Old and New* (Grand Rapids,
MI: Zondervan, 1982) makes the best of recent liturgical scholarship available and meaningful for a lay readership.

In relating worship to ethics, no one can ignore Geoffrey Wainwright's *Doxology* (New York: Oxford University Press, 1980). Beginning with the bold premise that worship shapes all Christian
life and thought, Wainwright constructs an entire systematic theology. In *On Liturgical Theology* (New York: Pueblo, 1984), Aidan
Kavanagh masterfully unfolds the liturgy on its own terms, dem-
onstrating how socially and politically relevant it naturally is.
Lastly, we mention William Willimon's *The Service of God* (Nashville, TN: Abingdon, 1983). Will Willimon is a working pastor, a
solid thinker, and a fine writer. The man's heart is in the church
and his book is to the point.

—Rodney Clapp

Index